Rohinton Mistry

Identity, Values and Other Sociological Concerns

Rohinton Mistry

Identity, Values and Other Sociological Concerns

Jagdish Batra

Prestige

an international publishing house

Published by
Prestige Books
3/28, East Patel Nagar
New Delhi 110 008
Ph. 9818755529
email: prestigebooks@gmail.com
website: asiabookclub.com
ISBN: 81-7851-038-3

Printed at Chaman Offset Press, New Delhi 110 002

Contents

for

Professor S.L. Paul

My Guide and Mentor

Chapter 1

Rohinton Mistry and His Works

When Rohinton Mistry selected the title of his second novel *A Fine Balance*, he articulated, consciously or unconsciously, his total approach to the world of letters. Not for him the flamboyance of style or hyperbolic generalizations of thoughts, instead he mastered the art of speaking his mind in the most humble though graceful manner, retaining the balance between subject matter and style as also between his involvement and detachment. While choosing the time-tested method of conventional story-telling, Mistry could very effectively communicate his point of view on the intractable complexities of life in India.

Rohinton Mistry as a fiction writer occupies an important place in Indian writing in English. Right from his first offering titled *Tales from Firozsha Baag*, it had become clear that Indian English fiction had got a very talented writer. Being based in Canada does not affect the depth of his insight into the Indian reality. The beauty of his works has ensured that on the literary firmament, he hogs limelight with the likes of V.S. Naipaul, Salman Rushdie, Vikram Seth et al.

Often compared to Charles Dickens for his compassionate realism, Mistry was born in Bombay (now Mumbai) on July 3, 1952. He graduated with a degree in Mathematics from the University of Bombay in 1974. He migrated to Canada the next year, where he got married to Freny Elavia, who had also studied in the same college in Bombay in which Rohinton was a student.

More than writing, Rohinton Mistry was interested in music and had performed in Bombay also. According to his own confession, he wanted to make a career in music in Canada and was successful in cutting an album of folk songs there. The music company Polydor released a disc labelled 'Ronnie Mistry.' However, he was destined to work initially at the Canadian Imperial Bank of Commerce and study part-time at the University of Toronto. In this way, he got his second degree in 1982.

Mistry wrote his first short story 'One Sunday' in 1983. It won him the First Prize in the Canadian Hart House Literary Contest. He won the same award the following year for his short story captioned 'Auspicious Occasion.' Again, in 1985, he bagged the Annual Contributors Award of the Canadian Fiction Magazine. All these prizes boosted his spirits and he left his bank job and became a full-time writer. A grant from the Canada Council made this changeover easy for him.

There started a new phase in his life in 1987 with the publication of a collection of short stories titled *Swimming Lessons and Other Stories from Firozsha Baag*. The stories revolve around a Parsi residential complex called the Khodadad building. The neighbourhood relationships as also individual lives have been patiently studied by the writer.

Four years later, he came out with his first novel *Such a Long Journey* based on the story of a Bombay bank clerk who becomes a victim of the scheming indulged in by the high and the mighty of the land. The novel was shortlisted for the prestigious Booker Prize. The Canadian Governor General's Literary Award for Fiction also came his way for this very novel. Two more awards followed the next year: These were the Commonwealth Writers Prize awarded to Mistry for this novel being the Overall Winner and the Best Book, and the Smith Books in Canada First Novel Award.

In 1995, he published his second novel titled *A Fine Balance* to the acclaim of the literary community in the form of the Giller Prize. Set in the period of the much-hated Emergency in India, the novel broadens the canvas to include the rural India with its dismally poor populace. The next year, this novel was shortlisted for the Booker. Another feather in his cap was the Commonwealth Writers Prize awarded to him in 1996. The novel was such a rage with the reading public that recognition came from various quarters in quick succession in 1997. *A Fine Balance* was shortlisted for the International IMPAC Dublin Literary Award as also for the Irish Times International Fiction Prize. The Los Angeles Times Book Prize (Fiction) was showered on it as also the Winifred Holtby Memorial Prize.

Mistry was well established by now and his third novel *Family Matters* published in 2002 was an instant hit. It tells the story of an old professor of English literature and underlines Mistry's essential humanism. The awards won by this novel included the Kiriyama Pacific Rim Book Prize (2002), the Canadian Writers Association Award for Fiction (2003) and the Timothy Findley Award (2006). Besides, it was also shortlisted for the International IMPAC Dublin Literary Award in 2004 and for the Man Booker Prize in 2002.

The locale of most of Mistry's fiction is the city of Bombay (now Mumbai) but since he left it at the age of twenty three only, one is bound to suspect his nostalgia at work here. Mistry's selection of the Parsi characters and the elaborate descriptions of their lifestyle and rituals etc. also points to this aspect.

Mistry's first collection of short stories *Tales from Firozsha Baag* brings together the stories written by him at the beginning of his career. Some of them were written without any thought of eking out a career as a writer, but even a conservative critic would fail to find any lacuna with regard to Mistry's art of storytelling. The *Tales* are based upon the day-to-day experiences of the residents of a decrepit apartment block Firozsha Baag in Bombay. Mistry brings together assorted characters—the elderly Rustomji, dubbed 'curmudgeon' for his penny-wise proclivities, the expert story teller Nariman Hansotia, the old and eccentric maidservant Jaakaylee, the wayward and voyeuristic lad Pesi, the contrasting siblings Kersi and Percy, the sadistic-though-pitiable hag Khorshedbai and many others.

Mistry has been able to bring out the strengths and weaknesses of relationships among the residents of the block. What is more, some of the characters are common to many stories as in case of Kersi, the teller of the stories 'Lend me Your Light' and 'Swimming Lessons.' He also plays an important part in 'One Sunday.' Of course, the little boy that Kersi is shown in 'One Sunday' has grown up to be independently settled in Canada by the time the other two stories are put in his mouth. Again, Najamai of 'One Sunday' also has a role in 'Condolence Visit,' though the role shifts from the central to the peripheral one. These repetitive appearances assure the reader that he stays within the precincts of the Firozsha Baag and chances upon meeting different characters as one actually does in such a locality. Seen from this angle, Mistry also displays a fine dramatic sense. Besides, the reader has an opportunity to get multiple views of the same character. This is Mistry's method of fortifying realism.

Such a Long Journey (1991), Mistry's first novel, won numerous literary awards when it was first published. It has since been made into a film also. The novel is set in 1971 during the period of the Indo-Pakistan war over the influx of refugees from the then East Pakistan. The war resulted in the break-up of Pakistan and creation of a new nation, viz., Bangladesh. The protagonist of the novel is no conventional hero. Gustad Noble is a bank clerk and a family man, a vulnerable figure whose world is still haunted by the war with China that took place in 1962. The fate of Gustad's family is closely bound up with that of the subcontinent. His daughter's illness and his son's refusal to go to the IIT in keeping with the dreams of his father, are events that the reader cannot but sympathize with but his life takes a terrible turn when he receives a parcel from an old friend Major Bilimoria, who requests him to deposit it into a fictitious account. The ramifications of this single money-laundering deed are at once personal and political. Henceforth start travails of this simple, and as the name suggests, noble-at-heart unheroic hero who emerges ultimately unscathed from these trying times.

A Fine Balance, critically Mistry's most successful and also the most voluminous work to date, tells the story of four characters—Maneck Kohlah, Dina Dalal, Ishvar and Omprakash, all of whom bear the brunt of Indira Gandhi's infamous state of emergency promulgated in the country in 1975. It is the story of impoverishment of the ordinary people whose voice would never reach the people occupying the top echelons of society. Mistry has shown his skill in portraying memorably poignant portraits of post-independence India. As is common to any unjust order, the powerful and the influential ultimately carry the day. The message sent out in this novel is terse and clear: the deep-rooted contentment of the Indian psyche is unbeatable. Whether one celebrates it or weeps over it is the outsider's problem, within this country, things just move on.

A strong indictment of the functioning of Indian leaders as this book is, it has justifiably aroused strong reactions. When *A Fine Balance* was announced as a Booker candidate, all hell broke loose. Speaking on a BBC program, the Australian writer and critic Germaine Greer was reported to have commented that she loathed the book as it was not based on reality and that this was "a Canadian book about India." Allegations of over-dependence of the writer on newspaper reports were freely hurled but these never really stuck to Mistry.

Mistry's latest novel *Family Matters* (2002) is based in Bombay once again. Whereas his first two novels were set in the decade of 1970s and were essentially inspired by historical events, the present novel depicts the Bombay of the 1990s. At the centre of the plot is an old man, a Parsi with Parkinson's disease. Nariman Vakeel is a retired academic whose illness places renewed strain on the family budget as also on the relations within the family. A widower with skeletons in his cupboard, Nariman imagines himself to be King Lear. The memories of his past expose the reader to earlier moments in the city's and the nation's history in a novel that moves across three generations of the same family.

In *Family Matters*, we have the familiar slippage between public and private worlds. Similarly, the lives of the residents of the Chateau Felicity (Nariman's former residence) and the Pleasant Villa (where he is deposited into the care of his daughter by a scheming step-daughter) recall the world of Firozsha Baag. But to rest content with portraying personal problems is not too satisfying a job for Mistry and so the damning environs created by the fanatic Shiv Sena in a hitherto cosmopolitan Bombay play their part and turn Nariman's son-in-law Yezad's life into hell for which he is also partly to blame. His culpability at this point becomes an interesting subject of study and Mistry's craftsmanship in creating a perfect psychological puzzle deserves accolades.

A common thread that runs through all his works is Mistry's concern for society. His works have been moulded by social reality and he too, in turn, has analyzed the situation like a sociologist and pointed out, within the boundaries set for an artist, the inadequacies and weaknesses of our social and political order.

Chapter 2

The Theoretical / Historical Framework

Rohinton Mistry's fictional works comprising of three novels and an anthology of short stories provide penetrating insights into the social reality of India. His penchant for realism subsumes his concerns for the fast-eroding value system in individual and public life, the endangered Parsi identity which he would flaunt with pride but which needs to be redefined and an essential humanism transcending its various labels and manifestations. Since he is a member of the Indian diaspora settled in Canada, he partakes of certain diasporic traits like nostalgia that further goes to recreate reality with liberal help from media-spun yarns. While admitting all this, one must not fail to give due allowance to him for his endeavours to understand events and various questions thrown up in this post-colonial world. Quite often, he betrays the proclivities of a sociologist or even a socio-psychologist. Before we venture into any effort to read various 'isms' and ideologies in his works, an examination of different approaches and theories should be in order at this stage.

The concern for social reality has moulded both—the writer and the critic—in the mould of sociologists in our times. This kind of thinking proceeds on the assumption that a language represents a society at the deepest level. This is similar to the manner in which psychologists discover hidden traces of an individual's personality in his dreams. Whitehead is not wide of the mark when he says that the humanity expresses its viewpoint in literature. Modern age academics debated for long whether literature ought necessarily to bother about society. In other words, was art to be for the sake of art alone? Whereas critics like Matthew Arnold were for art devoted to life, others like Walter Pater would rather have art for its own sake only. If we believe the latter viewpoint, then aesthetics and social values have to be treated as totally unrelated to each other.

The Greeks believed that art occupied a higher niche in the life of a community. For them, the aesthetics conformed to civic objectives. Aristophanes was of the view that comic poets not only provided joy to a community and moulded its taste; they also acted as the moral and political teachers of the community. Horace opined that literature must be useful and pleasant. In English literature, Sidney expressed the view that the final aim of all worldly learning was virtuous action and it was the duty of literature to foreground it. The Neo-classicists of the seventeenth and eighteenth centuries like John Dryden, Alexander Pope and Dr. Samuel Johnson stood for the twin objectives of instruction and delight in literature.

The Romantic Age began in 1798 with the publication of *Lyrical Ballads* by William Wordsworth and S.T. Coleridge. The Romantics sought to be guided by the inner voice rather than the classical rules, but here also they preferred the moral strain, which they claimed, could be imbibed from nature. Whereas Wordsworth believed each one of his poems had a moral purpose, Coleridge was of the view that the primary aim of literature was pleasure, truth being secondary.

Post-Marx, the attitude towards authorial objective has changed. If we approach ancient literature on the basis of patrons' influence on it, we shall find that in the Roman empire, famous poets like Virgil, Horace and Ovid relied on the magnanimity of heart of the ruling kings and emperors. This is not to deny the fact that during the Middle Ages, a number of monks and wandering bards or vagrant scholars also made their mark. Equally, it can be said of the church and nobility who supported special type of literature. A number of English poets and dramatists like John Dryden wrote to please the king. Some like Shakespeare could write well enough to please both the nobility and the groundlings, but besides writing what the latter wanted, Shakespeare could also write what they needed. In the eighteenth century, authors started earning handsomely from their writings and could forsake the royal patronage. Thus, Pope amassed much wealth and could write independently. Successful prose writers like Addison brought out their periodicals and wrote the way they wanted. This was the route to success taken by litterateurs like Voltaire, Goethe and Walter Scott.

The relationship between the society and the artist has lately been seen from the angle of the social and economic status of the writer and his family. While Russian literature before Chekhov was dominated by the aristocratic class, in America, it was the middle class professionals who produced literature. In England, it was mostly the sons of churchmen and workmen that took to writing. The question to be considered here is: Did it essentially leave any particular imprint on literature? For all we know, Byron belonged to nobility but his literature does not represent the interests of nobility. Same is the case with Pushkin and Shelley. Most of the court poetry of the seventeenth century was written by poets of lower order. So, it can be said that the social origins of a poet or a writer might—but just might, play a small role in shaping the ideology of their works. In contemporary times, a section of writers does resort to churning out pot-boilers. Ghost writers who work for monetary benefits also exist. But a natural genius and a successful writer like Rohinton Mistry is not suspected of having used his talents to that end. Of course, wild charges of selling an exotic India to the West are sometimes hurled at him but these fail to stick, such is the reputation of this writer.

Having referred to the impact of society on the writer, it must also be submitted here that the writer may also influence the society, although it is very difficult to gauge the exact extent to which this impact occurs. Thus, Rousseau's call for 'Liberty, Equality and Fraternity' is widely believed to have spurred the French Revolution. Joseph Addison's impact on the 'wives and daughters' of London as mouthed by the imaginary member of the Spectators' Club may not be a true indicator of the exact impact of his essays on the society of his times, but it cannot be denied that these must have had some influence on the thinking of the English middle class of that period. Mistry has fearlessly joined the ranks of those who condemned the imposition of Emergency rule in India. In his fiction, he has persuasively espoused the cause of his community, viz., the Parsis without inviting the wrath of the majority community. After all, his is a sane voice raised in favour of human rights and freedom.

A writer may, therefore, influence society and in turn be influenced by it. In other words, art may shape life and vice versa. When a writer comments on society, we have to be careful about the tone of the author. It could be realistic just as is desired in the case of a historical writer or it could be satirical if the writer means to disapprove of a certain state of affairs. It could be romantic (John Lyly's *Eupheus*) that could paint an idealistic picture of society. It is here that we feel the need to tap sources other than the literary ones only like political, social and economic treatises, to arrive at a fair picture of society. So, interpreting literary material requires caution and supplementation at times. Such a need may not be felt in case of contemporary novelists like Rohinton Mistry, but as will be seen, different viewpoints emerge even though far more efficient and keen watchdogs in the form of mass media exist now.

Sociological criticism covers the relationship between the author and the society. In this, it is different from historical criticism which relates literature to the history of a period. This criticism has its genesis in the eighteenth century work on Iliad (*La Scienza Nuvoa* by Vico) in which the critic related Homer to the spirit of his time. It is aptly believed that Homer composed *Iliad* when Greece was young and burning with 'sublime' passions such as pride, anger and vengeance, so that he then admired Achilles, the hero of force. Having grown old, he composed *Odyssey*, at a time when the passions of Greece were somewhat cooled down by reflection, which is the mother of prudence so that he now admired Ulysses, the hero of wisdom.

Thus, sociological criticism was essentially based on the concept of literature reflecting the society. It is different, however, from the view of the author as a moral leader because he was himself seen as a product of society or social forces. Some critics have pointed out that the geographical and climatic conditions fashion a work. How far this could be right is again a matter of conjecture because Southey, Coleridge and Wordsworth—all belonged to the same period and to the same part of England and yet the works produced by them are markedly different.

The twentieth century has not been very enamoured of the 'art for the sake of art' theories. This is borne out by the fact that even the surrealists, who appeared at the turn of the century, also claimed to serve a purpose. Similarly, Walter Pater, the chief exponent of the 'art for the sake of art' theory had to contend with "the power of literature for increase of sympathy, amelioration of suffering, service of humanity" in his 'Essay on Style.' Besides, there is a long list of the erstwhile supporters of this theory who went back on their words. The list includes the names of Baudelaire, Flaubert et al. Among the other leading critics, whereas Matthew Arnold's concept of the man and the moment held both the factors responsible for the creation of literature, T.S. Eliot laid equal stress on the tradition and the individual talent. F.R. Leavis's enunciation of sociological approach is remarkable in that it supplements new criticism that had cut literature off from life totally. In fact, the New Criticism was best suited for poetry. It is now widely appreciated that sociological critic should not bind an author to a particular creed like communism, capitalism etc.

The economic element was introduced by the Marxists. According to Karl Marx, art, literature and philosophy as also law and politics form the superstructure of state that is decided primarily by the economic structure of society. Marx was not so fastidious and also believed in author's influence on his times but his followers were more enthusiastic in this matter. Granville Hick, a Marxian, wanted literature to show class struggle with realistic portrayal of life from the point of view of the proletariat. In the 1920s and 1930s, ultra-Marxist authors held sway.

Again, the decade of 1950s saw an upsurge in sociological criticism, mainly of the Marxist inspiration. A leading role was played by Lucien Goldmann who had worked under the influence of the Marxist Hungarian philosopher Georg Lukacs. Goldmann saw literary works "not as the product of an individual genius but as the expression of a collective social awareness or world view (*vision de monde*), thus anticipating the "death of the author" announced ten years later by Roland Barthes. (Goodman 168). In his later work *Towards a Sociology of the Novel* (1975), he presented a homology between the structure of the modern novel and the market economy. Another important figure to emerge in the 1960s was the critic Pierre Macherey, who saw writers as necessarily working within pre-existing literary genres, conventions and ideological structures which underwent a process of transformation in the literary text. His later works stressed the political role of literature and of criticism as a means of propping up the state and strengthening the status quo.

The interest of the postcolonial literature in oppression during the colonial rule in a large number of countries around the world has sociological importance. This interest has continued even in the aftermath of liberation of these countries from the foreign yoke for the simple reason that the state apparatus has hardly undergone any meaningful change and it continues to be oppressive and reminiscent of the colonial system. Certain fundamental oppressive structures in class, gender and caste continue to be in place. Such practices are undertaken ostensibly in the name of homogenizing the populace, federalism or national stability, elide differences and perpetuate oppression of the marginalized groups—women, lower classes, castes etc. The tools used by postcolonialism are also from the domain of sociology.

Again, the postcolonial focus on identity formation in the age of globalization and on studying the dangers of neocolonialism is of sociological importance. In this, Rohinton Mistry's attempt to underline the minority status of the Parsi community in post-colonial India ought to be acknowledged. The identity question is of great concern to the community and its enlightened leaders for another reason also and that is the fast depleting numbers of the Parsis all over the world.

An interesting concomitant is the debate taking place in the academia on the issue of integrity of the author. The postcolonial critics' concern about marginality has led them to question state hospitality enjoyed by writers espousing the cause of marginal identities. This has further taken some to place experience over theory or the social activism over academic pursuits. Critic Mike Featherstone proscribes the activities of literary intellectuals on the grounds that "we have to raise the sociological objection against the literary intellectual's license in interpreting the everyday, or in providing evidence about everyday lives of ordinary people." Raymond Williams, on the other hand, describes culture as a whole way of life within which artistic and intellectual labour co-exist through necessary linkages with other social activities. (Gandhi 61-62)

There is a very thin line of division between sociological criticism and cultural criticism. Whereas sociological criticism focuses on the social aspect of life, cultural criticism includes the entire cultural domain. Since culture is also considered to be superstructure supported essentially by the economic structure, the market situation becomes relevant there. A feature like the mental make-up of the reader that helps a book to sell also becomes the area of study in that kind of criticism. A strict adherence to this point would mean that an author is only interested in selling his books and thereby earning profit. Even if we write off fame as a by-product of high sales volume, we shall have neglected the importance of self-gratification that comes with the realization that one has contributed one's mite to society by way of contributing constructive ideas or sensitizing people to certain values.

It may be safe to conclude that sociological criticism has undergone various changes since ancient times and the following perceptions are considered valid in contemporary times:

1. An author's work viewed as reflecting the social reality.
2. Author treated as a critic and a teacher of his age
3. Author considered as a product of economic forces.
4. Author considered as a product of the milieu of his time.

In fact, truth lies in each one of these viewpoints. The author is a product of environment—social, political, economic and historical but he is also a thinking individual, who has the power to shape his ideas and influence others. Based on this conclusion, it is logical to believe that what a writer writes is equivalent to the impact that society has made upon his mind but still scope remains for his initiative. He notes in his works the social reality and presents his suggestions for betterment and all this is deftly and aesthetically woven into the texture of his work. The problem for the critic is to recognize the author's voice from among a plethora of voices in a creative work.

With regard to Rohinton Mistry, the attempt in this book has been to give place to the varied viewpoints as discussed above. Our submission is that he has studied social reality in a remarkable manner and commented on it as a great intellectual and social thinker. He comes from a middle class educated Parsi background. Many years ago, he shifted from Mumbai to Canada, where he continues to work and live presently. He has seen the world and can easily compare things prevailing in India with what exists in several other countries. He has presented his viewpoint in an aesthetically appealing manner. He belongs to present times and what he has written about in his novels is by and large corroborated by the chronicles. This is, however, not to dismiss the charge levelled in postmodern times against historiography as suffering from myopia. There would always be scope for imagining for any author without which no work could be interesting enough for a reader. Apart from the gift of imagination, Mistry is blessed with a sharp intellect. He has obliquely commented on the unsavoury state of affairs prevailing in several walks of life in India. His concern is very genuine because of which his work has carried a rare appeal, not only for the Westerners for whom at times his writing seems to have been targeted, but also for Indians.

The sociologists study the social process in terms of the break-up of populace along well-articulated lines like those of religion, language, class, sex etc. Relationships among different groups starting with family and within the groups form another area of interest for them. Then there is the gamut of institutions and norms related to different areas of life like economic, political, educational etc. Most of the sociologists consider society as an organic whole which is always in a state of flux. There are the agents of change like legislature, technology, culture etc. Social change is a hard fact, although the measure and direction of movement is very difficult to gauge, as we have to deal with the human factor. Still, attempts have been made to provide a theoretical base to sociology. The progress theorists like Comte, Spencer and Marx and the cyclical theorists like Toyanbee, Spengler and our own ancient Indian thinkers have tried to define the direction of social change. Despite wide differences in the perceptions of these two groups, there is a consensual common ground which grants the scope for the march of society towards the goal set before it in the limited span of foreseeable future. In Mistry's works, one can see an attempt to understand society along these lines.

The concept of sociological criticism, as mooted by the Marxist scholars is to find out what exactly motivated a writer to write what he or she wrote. A writer is seen as a product of the social structure. He absorbs the social values unintentionally and even subconsciously. While studying his biological details, we focus on his formative influences. His own background and class ideology become relevant to sociological criticism. We know Mistry was born to a middle class Parsi family of Bombay and is now settled in Canada. In that sense, he should share a bourgeois mentality. He should be loath to identify himself with the proletariat or the underdogs and aspire to be one with the aristocracy. The fact is that during Marx's times, the phenomenon of profitable immigration from India to Canada had not picked up the way it has over the past few years, so that the traditional middle class dream of making it big is no big deal now.

On the other hand, the radical Marxists demand strict adherence to certain principles of writing. These include noting the class structure in a society and revealing the exploitation of the downtrodden by the economically well-off capitalists who own the means of production. It would be a great injustice to Mistry if we do not appreciate his delineation of the lot of the poor and the downtrodden. He has particularly fixed the spotlight on the lowliest of the lowly in a very impressive manner, in his novel *A Fine Balance*.

So far as the capitalist class is concerned, we do not see in Mistry's novels big industrialists living off the hard labour of the masses. Instead, we see the writer shifting the spotlight on to the entire socio-political structure in which the levers of power are monopolized by the elite. Dharmasi, though coming from rural area, has learnt the tricks of trade of the politicians and exploits the illiterate and poor masses ruthlessly.

The Marxist model, however, has its own limitations. We cannot exactly pinpoint a particular event in the life of a poet or an author and say that this is what motivated him to write such and such piece. If we believe in that dictum, we shall be depriving the author of any capability to think afresh or contribute any original ideas. This is not borne out in practice. The writer does contribute something from his side and does it genuinely and meritoriously. If it were not the case, the world would not have revered great literary personalities. Mistry does take note of the sordid and seamy side of life in India as would be clear from the discussion that follows. The criticism of life and his unease with the existing state of things is brought home in the manner of an artist, that is, indirectly and tangentially. Any artist, true to his trade, will certainly insist on conveying his message in the most unobtrusive manner. He is not a scientist, after all.

II

The sociological concerns of Rohinton Mistry also include his fascination for the cultural life of the Parsi community to which he belongs and which made India its home some centuries ago. The level and desirability of its adaptability to the Indian milieu is a question that needs probing. Apart from the dominant Hindu community, there are the communities like Muslims, Christians and so many others of native origin. The adaptability comes about through acculturation and assimilation. While the former involves the outward transformation, the latter—a far slower phenomenon—constitutes a search for home and a revised identity

Within the Indian populace, there are innumerable groupings of indigenous linguistic and religious denominations. The 'son of the soil' dogma does not merely operate at the political level, it also informs these socio-cultural formations. Under the circumstances, the indigenous faiths would put themselves on a higher pedestal than the one allowed to the 'outsiders.' The links between the ancient Persian civilization and the Indus Valley civilization as also the common ground in Sanskrit and Persian languages give a different colour to the relations between the Parsis and the Hindus. While these cultural bonds date back to pre-historic times, known history does not point to any element of violent compulsion in this interface. Such a historical trajectory is unavailable to the Hindu-Muslim as also the Hindu-Christian interface. For this reason, the image of the Parsis living in India has not received any significant dent on any front. And yet the rise of Muslim fundamentalism, in the aftermath of the Arab-Israel conflict had a domino effect among all faiths, in varying degrees. While some have used violent means, others have given vent to their feelings through accepted means of expression.

The question of identity has becomes very important for every community or grouping, more so if it has a minority character in these post-colonial, postmodern times. The word 'identity,' though so familiar and real, refers to different aspects of the great human race. According to the Oxford dictionary, identity, in an individual context, refers to "the sameness of a person or fact that a person or thing is itself and not something else." Personal identity has three basic components: a sense of personal distinctiveness, a sense of personal continuity and a sense of personal autonomy.

A person is supposed to have a strong sense of identity if he sees himself as different from other people or if he strives to be a self-consistent individual displaying continuity in his attitude, beliefs and actions or if he has the ability to act in an independent way, taking his own decisions. Such a person will feel his identity threatened if he is faced with a situation not favourable to anyone of the essential components of his sense of identity. Erickson observes that a sense of identity "is never gained or maintained once and for all. Like a good conscience, it is constantly lost and regained."

A person who pretends to an identity that he does not have or dissembles an identity that is not fundamental to him, often becomes neurotic, even schizophrenic. This feeling of split personality is both painful and troublesome. Having lost the sense of personal identity, such a man feels alienated and lonely and makes frantic efforts to seek, organize and affirm his sense of identity through his affiliation with the group of his choice to seek his acceptance and recognition as a member of a society. His commitment to definite values and beliefs in life will produce feelings of belongingness and security resulting in regaining a reaffirmation of his lost identity.

The existential questions have troubled man's mind ever since he appeared on this earth. In our part of the world, thinkers mused over the meaning of life and the relationship between man and nature. These musings led them into the realm of the supernatural and spirituality. Jawaharlal Nehru in his *Discovery of India* pays tribute to this questioning spirit of man that lies at the root of great spiritual works like the *Upanishads*: "The *Upanishads* are instinct with a spirit of inquiry, of mental adventure, of a passion for finding out the truth about things. The search for this truth is, of course, not by the objective methods of modern science, yet there is an element of the scientific method in this approach. . . . The emphasis is essentially on self-realization, on knowledge of the individual self and the absolute self, both of which are said to be the same in essence." (89)

The Vedas, by and large, contain prayers to the Almighty and a record of the progress of man in various fields like medicine, music, science etc. till the time of writing of these holy books. "In these holy scriptures, sublime thoughts suggesting purity of ideas, truthfulness of speech and nobility of action are embodied" (Chandavarkar 8). In contrast, in the *Upanishads*, the probings into existential questions go deeper. The *Uttar Mimansa* which embodies the Vedantic philosophy hinges on the basic formulation encapsulated in the aphorism "*Aham Brahamsmi*" or "I am Brahma (or God)," hinting thereby at the union in Whitmanian terms, between the soul and the oversoul. The great sages had ascribed the highest place to the self.

The deeper questions connected with the existence of man, soul, God etc. did bother Heraclites and Socrates in the western world as they did the philosophers of later generations. The Socratic questioning and Platonic wondering had a lot to do with the identity of man and his relationship to society and gods.

The Renaissance was a momentous event for Europe and by all accounts, it brought the Hellenic influence on art and literature and thereby on lifestyle and thinking of the people. Its offshoots in the form of Reformation and Enlightenment culminated in rationalism that went on to appropriate the basis of human thought. While the Christian philosophers, of all hues, were necessarily concerned about the spiritual uplift of man, the first great modern philosopher Descartes gave a real thrust to philosophy into what was to be known as the secular domain. After the pre-Christ Greek philosophers, this was the renewed non-religious endeavour that assigned to man an identity that was shorn of divinity.

The French Revolution, though initially a harbinger of the good tidings of Liberty, Fraternity and Equality, soon turned sour. Napoleon's adventures had nothing to do with the haloed ideals of the Revolution. It was implementation of the French imperialistic project, very much in tune with the early colonizing sprees of different European nations, particularly England. Out of the ashes of the Revolution, rose the new religion of nationalism which impinged on human identity. Man was to be known by his country rather than religion and across the political boundaries of Europe he stood divided. This identity attempted to take its place above other identities of race, class, colour, profession etc.

Armed with these considerations, the West launched its project of 'civilizing' the other regions of the world, which truly meant subjugating and exploiting the weaker nations. The colonizers practised brilliantly the art of euphemism, so the mission to colonize the weaker nations was dubbed the 'mission civilisatrice.' Keeping the colonies under firm control and exploiting the subjects to the hilt required understanding them, for knowledge has been and is the most powerful weapon to dominate others. The 'other' was now made the subject of study and an all-enveloping, difference-effacing identity was bestowed on him. Edward Said's concept of Orientalism tears the mask off the benevolent face of the colonizer. This was a one-sided affair and the colonized were not supposed to understand or codify the colonizer.

The postcolonials, as we know, raised their voice in the 1980s against the nationalist resistance to colonialism. The ground for opposition was that the basis of resistance was Eurocentric. This was so in the case of concepts of nation-state, democracy and models of economic development. But having done that, they did not revert to the native models or philosophies. Instead, they chose to tread the path of unbridled freedom, somewhat of Utopian type. This opposition was stretched to include issues such as gender, race, class and (in India) caste. It was argued that the decolonized states also continued with the precolonized repressive paraphernalia which depended upon the elision of differences. In the name of homogenization, they perpetuated oppression of the marginalized. The march continued and even what were once considered to be deviant categories such as the gays and the lesbians, were included. So, giving voice to the sections silenced earlier by the colonial as well as nationalist powers became the agenda of the postcolonial theorists.

This kind of treatment of different marginalized groups had the inherent danger of re-creating categories. Essentialising and homogenizing were suspect in the eyes of the postcolonials. It also disapproved of master narratives as figured out by the structuralists. The total emphasis now was on differences and particularities. So, from the general, the movement was towards the local. Instead of dealing with the subaltern en bloc, it looked into their local contexts and pointed out the differences, say, between the plight of the dispossessed of Africa of a particular timeframe and that of the Indians belonging to another temporal context. Thus, the differences brought about by space and time were recognized.

This threw open the entire gamut of knowledge for re-reading because it showed domination, repression and resistance during the colonial period. Every area of knowledge and practice, from art and architecture to law-courts and scientific paraphernalia, education system and civil codes—each one showed hegemony of colonial ideology. Uncovering of the subtexts showing differences, Othering, discrimination between the native and the colonizer became a critical concern of the postmodernist.

If domination is one aspect, the other is resistance or complicity on the part of the native. This led to certain types of effects on the identity of both. Thus, according to Bhabha, westernization and dehumanization, hybridization and ultra-nationalist identities are some of the effects. The colonizer can construct his identity only through the stereotype of the 'Other' which involves homogenizing and effacing of differences. Besides, the colonial discourse is ambivalent, as it fetishes unity with the native and yet fears the wholly Other nature of the native. Edward Said's concept of Orientalism is based upon the premise that the West arrogates to itself attributes like being rational, developed, superior and human-like, while it considers the East or the Orient as irrational, undeveloped and inferior. Said showed the slanted perception of the colonized.

The question of identity derives inspiration from these formulations. According to Spivak, identity is dispersed and not self-present. She rejects all notions of fixed subject or authentic identity. For her, the pure subaltern voice is very difficult to hear because the subaltern subject position is constructed out of the colonial discourse. Homi Bhabha, in his *The Location of Culture* points to the connection between cultural differences and growth of identities: "The move away from the singularities of 'class' or 'gender' as primary conceptual and organizational categories, has resulted in an awareness of the subject positions—of race, gender, generation, institutional location, geopolitical locale, sexual orientation—that inhabit any claim to identity in the modern world. What is theoretically innovative and politically crucial, is the need to think beyond narrative of originary and initial subjectivities and to focus on those moments or processes that are produced in the articulation of cultural differences. These 'in-between' spaces provide the terrain for elaborating strategies of selfhood—singular or communal—that initiate new signs of identity and innovative sites of collaboration, and contestation, in the act of defining the idea of society itself." (1)

One of the major issues in Rohinton Mistry is of self-representation. Quite a few Asian Americans have depended upon memories and histories of cultural achievements of a by-gone era. A postmodern writer is supposed to be a different species since his immigration is not imposed but a voluntary one and he is expected to acquire a double vision in the bargain. It would be unjust to write off the cultural shock that an immigrant receives to start with, in his adopted country. That indeed arouses nostalgia in him which may not equal the magnitude of the writers of his preceding generations so that he does not need to reconstruct his original identity based upon memory. But all the same, it does leave a trace. Mistry himself felt such a shock when upon landing on the soil of Canada, he happened to listen to his favourite western music but then "living in the West made that same music seem much less relevant" (Gera 14). In his story 'Swimming Lessons,' his protagonist is reminded of a glorious past by his parents, though Kersi, Rohinton Mistry's alter ego by all accounts, does not go by that advice so that a trace is left in the postmodernist deconstructive sense. The story also talks about the life of a Canadian family which, coming from the pen of an Indian immigrant, presents a mirror-image of Orientalism.

The postmodern world is marked by global trade and voluntary immigration, diaspora and mixed identities. While the modernist view treated the agent as free to forge his own subjectivity, he was supposed to have choices and was himself held responsible for his actions. His identity was supposed to be coherent, but the postmodern view of identity dislocates this so-called 'mature modernist identity' dubbing it an "anachronistic modernist sham" (Butler in Baral 73) and looks upon all identities as functional and not absolute. Contrived to facilitate social commerce and inter-action, these are not stable, permanent and continuous, rather these are contingent, relational, fluid and ephemeral. According to the psychoanalytical theories also, the agent is conflict-ridden and self-deluded. Foucault, on the other hand, made the constitution of the inner self dependent upon the outside world of power and discourse.

Jacques Derrida, the high priest of deconstruction, also viewed identity as fractured and decentred. His observation makes it clear: "All that a deconstructive point of view tries to show is that since conventions, institutions and consensus are stabilizations. . . . This means that they are stabilizations of something essentially unstable and chaotic. Thus, it becomes necessary to stabilize precisely because stability is not natural; . . . it is because there is chaos that there is need for stability. If there were continual stability, there would be no need of politics, and it is to the extent that stability is not natural, essential or substantial, that politics exists." (Dallmyr 22)

The civilizing mission of the West has taken on the contemporary garb of globalization which clearly applies Western parameters of success and failure to the 'others.' The war against terrorist organizations inimical to the West is portrayed as being in universal interest. Thus Samuel Huntington's reductive phrase of 'the west and the rest' makes the intention clear. This is in tune with the broader pattern to obliterate individual differences and identities and to foist a homogenising universal West-inspired identity. The postmodern project specifically aims at deconstructing this phenomenon and presents clearly the parts that make up the whole.

Traditionally, human subject has been considered to be autonomous entity independent of all contingencies, self-sufficient and capable of leading isolated lives. Post-Hegel, individual identity has been seen as being dependent upon recognition by the other. It is now generally accepted that the identities are formed as a result of response of individual to society, arising out of cultural inter-relations. According to the relational theories of identity, which see the agent as both thinking and feeling individual responding to a complex of socio-historical and cultural factors and refuse to recognize the disembodied self of the spiritual domain, the role of society in forming identity can be casual, partial or total depending upon psychological attitude, mental capacity and value orientation of the agent. These identities are formed by social links such as language, tradition, history, norms and practices etc. It is a dialogical process rather than a unilateral or monological one. Identity depends upon a complex of social, physical, historical, economic, cultural circumstances. Since the circumstances are prone to change, so the self is also changeable and indeterminate.

While the subject is assigned certain identities of race, colour and gender at the time of birth, there are other identities dependent upon contingencies like economic class. Identities of religion and political affiliation can be placed in both the categories, which like Eliot's Prufrock, have ample time for revision. Social identities are constituted on cognitive, moral and aesthetic considerations. According to Bruner, self must be treated as a construction that "proceeds from the outside in as well as from the inside out." (Bruner in Naik 70)

Before concluding, a word about the feminist perspective should be welcome. The contemporary feminists find fault with almost all theories of identity because these are male-centric. They find the female subject as rational and coherent. They believe: "Individuals are formed through a complex interaction that is played out between the self and other, between consciousness and unconsciousness, between an always, already socially situated self and the society which helps to shape us, forming the background against which we act out our responses, subversions and have an objection to the self-centred image of the agent" (Mackenzie and Stoljar in Naik 72). Besides, they refuse to accept the view that subjects are self-centred as it goes against historical facts about women's lives, dedicated as they have always been to family. Instead of a strong sense of self, feminism promotes interdependence and inter-connection. Therefore, "the autonomous view of agent devalues women's experience and those values arising from it such as love, trust, loyalty, friendship, responsibility, caring and nurturance, particularly the mother-child relationships." (Naik 75) The character of Dilnavaz as presented by Rohinton Mistry in *Such a Long Journey* fits well in this groove whereas Dina Dalal of *A Fine Balance* shows some masculine sensibilities as she asserts her individuality.

Multiple identities in postmodern times also mean more internal conflicts, divided loyalties and cleft personalities. Conversely, these might make demands on individuals and goad them to bring to light their dormant potential. This occurs with a vengeance where the structures are oppressive. Socialization helps shape our identities and imbue a sense of commitment to social values. But at the same time, the individual identity cannot be totally written off, for in relation to society, it has a double-edged character: it affects others while it is itself affected in conscious or unconscious manner as an individual progresses along in this world and experiences life.

Rohinton Mistry's engagement with the identity problem is informed by the historical experience of his community. After the Parsis' exodus from ancient Iran, their settlement in Gujarat, their hobnobbing with the master race—all these left marks on their cultural identity. While during the Raj days, the western lifestyle and mores permeated the eastern inheritance of the Parsis, post-independence, sense of alienation possessed the Parsis. A large number of young Parsis continue to migrate to the west, Mistry himself being one of them, hoping to recover a life of comfort and pride. To re-create an identity with this kind of historical baggage in the contemporary fast-moving and fast-globalizing world is indeed a Herculean task, which Rohinton Mistry's three novels, viz., *Such a Long Journey, A Fine Balance* and *Family Matters* and a collection of stories entitled *Tales from Firozsha Baag* undertake effectively.

Rohinton Mistry's corpus is concerned more with the collective than the individual identity. The Parsis, as portrayed in his fiction, come out as feeling insecure, so far as their identity is concerned. That should not be taken to mean that his characters do not have any individuality. The main protagonists of his novels, whether it is Gustad or Yezad in *Such a Long Journey* and *Family Matters* respectively, are in the psychic dilemma of their own identity as they consider themselves to be minorities or second class citizens. Identity is the most vital question in their day-to-day life and it controls even the basic requirements of food, clothing and shelter, besides their world-view and perception of life. The Parsis want their next generation to inherit everything that is *Parsipanu* or related to the Parsi culture and ethos but then the members of the Gen-next—Jehangir, Murad, Sohrab, Darius, Percy, Kersi, Peshotan—have their own ideas and may not toe the line taken by their elders.

Enquiry along these lines inevitably invites the tag of roots-search. While Mistry does not dabble much in exploring the prehistoric or the historic past in his novels (there are brief references to the mythical and historical figures though), he does show his seriousness in searching for Parsi identity. Its location in lifestyle and various cultural exhibits like religion become his obsession at times. In every work, Mistry devotes considerable space to describing the system of Parsi prayers and rituals.

The Parsis have to their credit one of the oldest civilizations on this earth. "The word Parsi means the man from Pars or Fars, ancient parsa, Greek Persepolis, in southern Iran. The word Iran derives from the Avestan, *Airyana*, Sanskrit *Arya-yan*, the path or way of the Aryans. Hence *Iya-an*, abbreviated to Iran." (Nanavutty 1) The people of ancient Iran belonged to the Indo-European branch of the Aryans and their history goes as far back as 2000 B.C., when Zarathustra, the Prophet of ancient Iran is believed to have been born. A brief perusal of the ancient Parsi history throws in bold relief the Indian connection.

The Kayanian Dynasty ruled the Aryans of Iran till 700 B.C. The names of some of the kings of the period such as Kava Husravah, Kava Usa and Kava Vishtaspa find mention in *Rig-Veda* also. It is said to be a heroic period of the Iranian history. Later, the Achaemenian dynasty expanded the state into a vast empire. Some of the great figures of the time are Cyrus the Great (559-530 B.C.) and Darius (522-486 B.C.) who is said to have introduced banking, an activity in which the Parsis are still known to have a special expertise.

When Emperor Constantine embraced Christianity, a war started between Iran and Rome. Later, within the country, strife became the order of the day for quite some period. Great figures of the time that have their names etched on the minds of the common Parsis are Shapur I and Khushrau I who is better known as Nowshirwan-i-Adil (meaning Nowshirwan, the Just). Interaction with India started during this time. There is record of marriages between the royal families of the two nations as also interest in Indian music.

In 614 A.D., Khushrau II, attacked Jerusalem and captured it. Some 50000 Christians are believed to have been killed. Naturally, it enraged the entire Christian world. The Christian forces waged counter attacks. These were turbulent times for ordinary people who suffered untold miseries. This was also the starting point of decline of the Persian Empire. After the death of Prophet Mohammad, the Arabs started a series of invasions on Iran and were successful in capturing it in 641 A.D. The last king of the

Persian empire Yazdegard was in hiding for ten years before being caught and assassinated. The followers of Zarathustra had to flee, get converted or lie low.

The exodus to India started after a century or so. The documentary evidence speaks of a stream of migrants from 785 to 1021 A.D. However, trade and cultural relations between India and the Persian empire existed since, at least, the third century A.D. According to *Kissa-i-Sanjan* written in Persian by Dastur Sanjana, the migrating Parsis were received by the king of a coastal region in Gujarat—Jadhav Rana, who gave them permission to settle down on certain conditions. These included explaining the Zoroastrian faith to the king, the adoption of Gujarati as their mother tongue and sari as the dress by their women folk, the surrender of all weapons and carrying out of Parsi wedding ceremonies only during night so as not to offend the local sensibilities. The Parsis agreed to all these conditions.

According to a Parsi folklore sung in the form of garba songs, the king received the migrants in the presence of all local citizens. The head of the Parsi group, a priest, asked for permission to worship freely, to bring up their young ones according to their traditions and land to cultivate. These conditions were agreed to by the king who asked what they would do in return for the country. Upon this, "the old priest asked for a brass bowl to be filled with milk and brought to the assembly. This done, he stirred a spoonful of sugar in the bowl and holding it up in his trembling hands, said, 'We shall try to be like this insignificant amount of sugar in the milk of your human kindness.'" (Nanavutty 40) The king was touched by this humble submission and allowed them to stay. The Parsis have faithfully kept their word since and looked upon India as their motherland.

Barring a few bloody clashes with some jealous native tribes, this East-East interface, so to say, progressed well. Primarily, both Indians and Parsis belonged to the Indo-European branch of the Aryans. Their language and religious practices had a lot in common. Words like *Usa, Kavi, Gaumata* are from the ancient language of the Parsis. The favourite drink of the Aryans *soma* seems to have become *hauma* due to pronunciation problem just as the people of the Sindhu valley civilization were referred to as Hindus by the Arabs. Now, of course the Parsis speak Gujarati with a smattering of Persian words. Mistry has consciously used typical Parsi words as such in his writing.

The worship of fire, feeding it with sandalwood branches, is quite similar to the Vedic *Yajna*. In fact, according to a school of thought, the idea of fire as a god was brought by the Magis from Persia. The marriage ceremony benedictions are recited in Sanskrit even now. The Gayatri *mantra* and the Trishtubh prayer have a lot in common. The Parsi *Gathas* expound some obscure words of the *Rig-Veda* on the basis of certain archaic grammatical forms. The *Kusti* which every Parsi must wear as a distinctive mark can be compared with the *Yagyopaveet* worn by the Hindus. Both these items mark the first initiation ceremony of a child into the fold of his respective faith.

Uprooted from the ancient Persia, where they ruled the land since times immemorial, they had an almost comfortable stay of a millennium in India. During the pre-independence days, the Parsis came in contact with the ruling European classes and struck rapport with them, driven by needs of commerce. They had an enterprising and adventurous spirit no less than that which fired the Europeans when they reached this part of the globe. But then the Parsis knew this region and its people better. They had also crossed the seas to establish trade ties with China, Burma and other countries of South East Asia.

By and by, the intimacy between the Parsis and the English deepened to such an extent that it landed the Parsis into the role of arbiters in many a commercial conflict between the English and the Dutch. On the cultural front, this led to the westernization of the Parsi community, a detailed account of which would be found later in this book. In a nutshell, "The Parsees dressed like the Europeans, smoked, drank, played cricket and pursued English education but the inner Parsee life remained unchanged" (Kumar 17).

But when the struggle for freedom from the British yoke began, quite a few among the Parsis enthusiastically took part in it. One cannot forget that it was Madame Bhikhaji Rustom Cama (1861-1936) who worked in exile for the cause of Indian nationalism and unfurled the first Indian national flag on foreign soil. Dadabhai Naoroji headed the Congress as the first native Indian. Parsis like Sir Pherozeshah Mehta, Sir Dinshaw Wacha and much later Minoo Masani walked like titans on the political stage of the country.

In other areas in post-independence India, nobody can forget Field Marshal Sam Maneckshaw under whose over-all command, the Indian army won the battle of Bangladesh. Some of the most famous business houses—Tata, Godrej, Wadia are household names in India. Homi Jehangir Bhabha is looked upon as the first nuclear scientist of India. Zubin Mehta has earned fame as a leading musician of the western school of music. Nani Palkhiwala and Soli Sorabjee have achieved heights in the legal profession. C.R. Irani and R.K. Karanjia have been leading journalists of the country. So many others have made their mark in other areas of activity that mentioning the names of all of them would not be possible here.

The reference to their contribution to the literary field, however, cannot be missed. Keki Daruwalla, Gieve Patel, Adil Jussawalla, Firdaus Kanga, Farrukh Dhondy, Rohinton Mistry, Saros Cowasjee, D.F. Karaka, Ardashir Vakil, Boman Desai, Dina Mehta, Nergis Dalal, Bapsi Sidhwa are some of the leading names in literature. All these symbols of achievement should give the Parsis adequate strength to hold their head high. They have created an image of honest, hard-working, sincere people endowed with business acumen and professional competence, which travels much like genes in their successive generations.

However, despite the best of contribution made by them to society, they know too well the pain of displacement. In the present set-up, politics is all about vote bank and they know that in terms of votes, their community stands nowhere. They live on the fringe of society in India and have doubts about the future of their race.

In contemporary times, the lure of the lucre (before the dollar lost its sheen—lately, that is) has attracted Indian youth to the western shores. There is no compulsion for the Parsi youth to leave India but the magnetism of the Western economy coupled with loss of political clout in this country has ushered in movement of the Parsi youth to the West. While most of the elderly Parsis approve of it or wink at it, a thinking Parsi dreads the prospect of being a gypsy. All this boils down to what is very well analyzed by Salman Rushdie in his *Imaginary Homelands*: "Our identity is at once plural and partial." (15). This problematization of ethnic identity has been very competently and beautifully taken up by Rohinton Mistry in his oeuvre.

The fascination for foreign shores seen lately in the young Parsis need not call for alarm *per se* when placed in the context of majority of well-educated Indian youth. The only concern that it causes to the Parsi community is the gloomy prospect of further decline of their numbers in India. A rough estimate of their population places them in the ratio of 0.016% of total population of India. Late marriages and obsession with upward mobility in profession means unwillingness to take on the responsibilities of parenthood. So, whether here in India or out there in the West, the number of the Parsis continues to go down. So far as their population in Iran or Pakistan is concerned, the less said the better.

III

Satire has always been hailed as a valuable tool in the hands of litterateurs who have used it to condemn those intellectual, moral or philosophical constructs of the age which did not appeal to them. In *A Fine Balance*, as in other works, his characters, even though illiterate rural people, can see through the antics of the politicians ranging in stature from a local politico Dharamsi to the Prime Minister of the country. In this, his fiction firmly establishes him as a votary of values. And the value system is not only valid for the domain of politics but also for the domains of personal and other categories of social action.

What are referred to as values in secular and liberal terms have hitherto been part of ethics or moral philosophy that has ordinarily been regarded as a normative science. Its problem is defined as the exact determination of the conditions which must be fulfilled if human will and action are to be made 'moral.' In this sense, it can be termed as the art of conduct. But the question that begs the answer here is what is moral just as Pilate asked "What is truth?" and did not wait for an answer before pronouncing Christ guilty. We can either declare some conduct as moral arbitrarily or we shall have to go back to historical development of the concept of moral judgement. We could also juxtapose a particular instance of conduct as it was exhibited alongside the imagined one which was expected.

Ethics teaches man how he ought to will. It is the science of the ultimate good that tries to find out ideals in human behaviour. It critically examines the right and wrong actions in the light of the ultimate good besides presenting moral ideals before man. In one way, ethics is related to human psychology because the will is the area of study of psychology. Unless we understand the process of willing—motives, desires, intentions, thoughts, feelings and their inter-relations, we cannot truly appreciate the inclination or disinclination towards the domain of values. Psychology shows the path to put into practice the moral ideals but the total moral situation is taken into consideration when moral judgement is to be passed. Moral values are unique and occupy highest place in the realm of values. Comments a critic, "Truth, beauty and goodness are the moral (also spiritual) values which taken together, generate the highest or ultimate value—self-realization. Self-realization is the highest value which gives appropriate value to all temporary, extrinsic and instrumental values." (Banerjee 264)

The history of normative judgment of human conduct is very old. It lies buried in religious ideas and practices and customary usages and rules of social intercourse which are as old as the society itself. At a very early stage of civilization, these influences put a constraint upon the individual. His actions are largely subjected to outside control and his life follows a definitely prescribed course of action. It is not till various regulatory factors are split up into well-defined groups that we find religion, custom, law and morality as different bodies of normative codes. Beyond this lies the demand for separate scientific investigation of different classes but the reflection of religion is expressly found in all human categorization. Even Socrates mentions two sources of moral order—the written laws of the state and the unwritten laws of the gods.

It was the later degradation in society all around him that propelled Socrates to look deeper into the problem and he came to regard virtuous or moral conduct as the result of knowledge, something that could be communicated and taught. It goes, however, to his credit that he provided, first of all, a rational basis to ethics, to wit, its utility to the state. Plato, like his master, tried to determine the conditions of the universal validity of moral standards. He considered virtue to be of universal validity because all that was good, came from God. The full realization of virtuous endeavour requires a certain kind of society or the state. In his *Republic*, Plato describes the special conditions under which mankind might live a life that should satisfy all the requirement of human nature.

Post-Aristotelian stoics favoured virtuous life as the highest good and aimed at a rational human endeavour. Epicureans considered social rules good because these provided individual with security. So, both these philosophical schools found justification for ethics of their times. How times define their faith in values can be gauged from the fact that both Plato and Aristotle "defend slavery and both are influenced by national prejudices; both look upon 'barbarians' as inferior peoples and upon slavery as a natural and just institution." (Thilly 115)

Christianity introduced an entirely new point of view, characterized by three principal ideas: the idea of inevitable guilt, the command to love all men and the belief that future blessedness or condemnation is necessarily determined by the moral quality of the life lived upon earth. According to the Christian theology, no man can attain to a guiltless life; the original sin sits so heavy on all. Since all human beings have been created by God, they are brothers in guilt. Jesus is the son of God through whom redemption may be sought. Christianity was known for its emphasis on love and repentance. It laid out a system of rewards and punishment by way of heaven and hell for the virtuous and the sinning respectively. Christianity also started the debate about the freedom of human will. The ideas of merit and guilt, so strongly emphasized, had no meaning unless man had freedom of choice.

St. Augustine epitomizes the Christian approach to ethics. For him, love united man with God, the highest good. So, love was the supreme virtue and the source of all other virtues. It taught man other values like self-discipline and temperance because the latter stands for this world. "Without love faith can do nothing; nor is love without hope, nor hope without love, nor either without faith," he declared.

The Reformation, in the wake of the Renaissance, revived interest in ethics. The asceticism and the escape from the world had characterized the middle ages. Now, the belief in the vocation in the world was looked upon as satisfying all the requirements of a moral life. It was now believed that our work in the world had a positive side to it and that pleasure in earthly matters is permissible since the world and all that is in it had come from God. Along with this conviction went a deepening of the religious sentiment. Not by any outward works can we acquire a claim to happiness, but only by a steadfast inward faith that triumphs over the world and if we lack this faith, no outward ceremony may give us freedom or redemption from guilt. He, who will be moral, is thus taught to look to himself. His regeneration must take place within himself, his fight with the evil power of sinful passions is an inward conflict and only faith in God and His mediator Christ can assure him courage, joy and peace.

The reflective spirit characterized the ushering in of the modern age. It meant the revolt against authority and tradition and a demand for freedom of thought, feeling and action. Since the political conflict between the Pope and the state in the European countries was settled in favour of the state, state replaced church as an organ of civilization. Nationalism and not the ecclesiasticism was the reigning creed now. And the state stood for democratic institutions rather than absolutist kings. The doctrine of political non-interference in the affairs of the individuals was to be guarded with jealousy henceforth. At the same time reason became authority in science.

Benedict Spinoza, the great Dutch philosopher, is known for his pantheism but he looked at virtue from a different angle. He considered it power and in a way, linked ethics to politics. But he also stressed the importance of reason on which depended finally one's happiness. This also led to consideration of others' welfare. So, morality became a matter of enlightened self interest for him. This very thinking influenced Locke and his followers.

The German philosopher Leibniz, the propounder of 'the best possible world' theory, believed that moral instincts were inherent in man. These were weakened by passion. Another great German philosopher Kant put forth his doctrine of the categorical imperative and opined that one must do right for the sake of right alone. A moral man was worthy of happiness but he must not undertake right actions for the sake of happiness.

Coming to various ethical virtues, whereas Herbert found five grounds to rest the ethical system upon, Schopenhauer zeroed in on sympathy or pity as the most cardinal virtue. In fact, every philosopher of any standing has had to reckon with the issue of ethics. The consideration of good has always guided philosophers so much so that different systems of philosophy interpreted reality in terms of what ought to be rather than what was or is. In a way, it is appropriate, for man is not made to see reality as chaotic. Ethics occupies the pride of place even in the age of science. Ever since the enlightenment period, modern ethics has endeavoured to obtain a universally valid basis for moral standards. In this, even Mathematics has been sought to be made the basis of ethics. But that was a superficial method followed by Spinoza, Hobbes, Locke et al. Modern philosophy has evolved the following bases for scientific ethics:

1. Different from religion and metaphysics, empirical scientific treatment of moral questions was advocated.
2. If based on some existing empirical science like psychology, biology, political economy, it automatically becomes scientific.
3. Identified with the touchstone of utility to individual or community, it becomes precise.

These distinctions are in the ideational or abstract domain. At the practical level, they are all clubbed together. Efforts have been made to put ethics on independent foundation because by leaning upon psychology, or political economy or sociology or any other science, it will not become a universally valid discipline. For this, it should evolve its own stand based upon facts which are peculiarly its own, and are accessible only to its methods. Only then it could be called scientific ethics.

Ethics is essential. When Locke proceeded on the assumption of a purely selfish individual, he found that the wills of all clashed with one another's. Social life and peace become possible only when there is a "reasoned and calculating compliance of each with the demands of all." Locke also believed in "three different types of law: the law of God, the law of the state and the law of public opinion. Hence, there must be three different forms of moral conduct. Under the divine law, action is dutiful or sinful; under the law of the state, guilty or innocent; under the law of public opinion, virtuous or vicious." (Pandit 52)

In fact, no one disputes that certain requirements, laws, norms of some kind etc. have their place in the consideration of human conduct. The contents of an ethical order may be different but the form of law or regulation has universal validity. The direction of the ethical order is decided by the needs, customs and opinions of a particular time. Different types of ethical systems exist in the world and the difference is mainly based on the following considerations:

1. The ethical systems that look for the origin of morality in the individual himself. The inner voice is the determinant for them. The standard of comparison for our actions is provided by that inner voice in the form of inner freedom, justice, benevolence and perfection and recompense.
2. Those that look to some outside authority for sanction. Such an authority could be religious, social or political. So, religion or state are the sanctioning bodies here.
3. An ethical system could appeal either to feelings and emotions or to reason and understanding.

With the gradual secularization, so to say, of ethics, we now enter upon a period in which values are backed by societal opinion rather than moral rules backed by religion. Ethics stands divorced from religious values though for some, religious values may narrow down to ethical ones only. Even spiritual values are differentiated from religious ones as the latter come from particular forms of organized religions.

We have a plethora of values: economic values, physical values, scientific values etc. There are the permanent and the temporary or the ultimate and the instrumental values besides the division of individual and social values. When we place moral values in the gamut of values, we feel that this naïve or intentional trickery of semiotics has upset the conventional order. It would suggest putting at par the moral values with the others though still predominant view is of placing moral values above others when it comes to giving them their due place in this spectrum.

Different people have different reasons to stick to the values of their choice. To a theist, only spiritual value is the highest because it brings him nearer to divinity, whereas to a materialist the value that brings him physical pleasure and material comfort is supreme. Since the parameters of pleasure change from individual to individual, such values are bound to differ. Spiritual values are logocentric and therefore stable. But values without any spiritual basis or religious sanction are likely to be violated easily.

Since ancient times, literature has been preoccupied with morality. The major concern of a modern litterateur is to be faithful to reality. This emphasis on realism drives him to paint in his works what actually is while the moral vision seeks for what ought to be. In the case of great many authors, both realism and a moral vision inform their creative works. But a writer's point of view has to be analysed carefully so as to segregate these two concerns because an author is the ventriloquist behind all voices in his work.

If we refer to Indian philosophy, which is primarily a philosophy of values, we find utmost place given to reverence for all forms of life, whether of human, animal or plant variety. Besides, the importance of human life has been underlined by juxtaposing it with eighty four lakh others births (*yoni*). This is very significant in the sense that it leads one to place a premium on values such as respect for others, democracy, equality, peace, social harmony etc. This reverence for life also demands a measure of tolerance for the viewpoints of others. Other important Indian human values include *Purushartha* (*dharmarthkamokshanam*) which guides the course of human life in this world. Dharma is the gateway to all desires and ambitions and *Moksha* is the climax of human endeavour.

The concept of Dharma is indeed a unique contribution of India to the world. The word religion literally means 'to bind' or 'to connect,' whereas Dharma has different interpretations that cover a very wide field. Dharma stresses duties and enjoins upon man to change himself. Therefore, it concerns what is more basic. What is in jeopardy is the gamut of moral values. The old adage 'If character is lost, everything is lost' holds good in the context of our present-day society. Now, these moral values stand intertwined with spiritual ones in Dharma, which alone can effectively instill them in man. The *Manusmriti* enumerates the following ten aspects of Dharma:

Dhriti kshama damosteyam shauchindiryanigraha
Dhir vidya satyakrodha dashkam dharmalakshnam.

(Patience, forgiveness, austerity, non-stealing, purity, control of senses, intellect, knowledge, truth and avoidance of anger are the ten symptoms of Dharma.)

Surprisingly, this description does not hinge on belief in God. As such, it should even be acceptable to an atheist. What is to be marked here is that the Indian value system deals with the fundamental human values. The dimensions of Dharma as given above agree with the basic principles of all religions.

Dharma is also to be differentiated from external rituals, signs and practices like ablution, *choti*, castration, pilgrimage etc. These might have their symbolic value but they do not have any intrinsic worth. Most often, they lead to social disharmony and conflict. Dr. S. Radhakrishnan calls dogmas and rites as 'necessarily inadequate symbolism' (186) in the religion of the spirit. One is free to adopt the way to worship Him. What carries weight are the values referred to in the aforesaid verse. Dharma is the golden link that connects man to God, *Atman*, society and nature.

The Parsi value system is based on their faith, viz., Zoroastrianism, which has been compared by Kulke to the Calvinist economic ethics because the former propagates an active pursuit of economic ends, something which the Parsis have always done with a gusto. In this, they come nearer the followers of the Sikh faith. Their history strengthens this viewpoint. They have always excelled in economic and business activities. Even in eighteenth century, Jamshedji Bamanji Wadia "built battleships and frigates for the Royal Navy, as well as merchant ships for the East India Company." (Nanavutty 86)

Zoroastrianism does not believe in casteism. The Parsis attach great value to righteousness, integrity and universal brotherhood. They believe in one God (*Ahura Mazda*). To prophet Zoroaster were revealed the various tenets of their faith. He did not favour any ritualism but with the passage of time, it has seeped into the Parsi faith. Zoroastrianism finds dualism in creation and looks upon the clash between the good and evil inevitable. *Asha* denotes the divine principle of righteousness, justice and harmony. A life of strict regimen leads to the reunion of man with God—a position that comes very near Indian Yoga. *Druj* is the Devil's way. While in the Indian system, we have *sattva, rajas* and *tamas* as the different states of mind, in Zoroastrianism these are referred to as *mainyus—spenta mainyu* or the higher spiritual self-consciousness which leads to *humata, hukatha and huvarstha* or good thoughts, good words and good deeds and *angra mainyu* or the lower self-consciousness which leads to *dushmata* or evil deeds.

While studying Rohinton Mistry's works against the backdrop of the domain of values, it is natural to look for answers to questions like:

1. Which individual, familial, social and communal values does he propound?
2. Does he denigrate any values as weak, dogmatic, outdated or impractical?
3. Does he pit individual against social values?
4. Which sanction does he approve of to back his favoured values?
5. Is he for ethics unrelated to religion? If not, which religion is he most impressed with—Hinduism, Zoroastrianism or any other?

It would be seen that his value system synchronises with humanism at its best. It should not be taken to mean that he denigrates his own faith Zoroastrianism. In fact, he goes great lengths to give details of Parsi rituals even as one can mark an underlying sense of distrust of these ceremonies on his part. Apart from these external details, he does not give any deep analysis of Parsi tenets. His approach to other religions is not narrow-minded or sectarian but liberal and humane, which places him in the company of Charles Dickens and Tolstoy.

This kind of humanism is faulted by some of the contemporary writers influenced by Marxism. Whatever the claims and counter-claims about humanism, one thing on which all seem to agree is that humanism is meant to upstage the human being. It does not hold any other ideology superior to the interest of the human being. Man is to be placed at the centre of all constructs. This universe is for his sake and if any action is detrimental to the interest of man, then it is fit to be shunned.

While studying Rohinton Mistry, one is struck by the writer's enlightened concern for the underdog and the downcast. His realistic portrayal of life in Indian villages with its problems of caste prejudices, serfdom, lack of amenities etc. in *A Fine Balance* shows his concern for the human being. Similarly, he speaks of the city slum-dwellers and their hellish life. There is focus on the pavement dwellers, crowded local trains, noise and pollution, dirt and squalor that is evident all around in any Indian city. The Indian middle class also finds wide mention in his fiction. The people belonging to this class are the ones who hang between two worlds—one at the bottom which they hate to identify with and the other at the top which they aspire to be with but fail miserably to achieve. In all cases, it is the human being that is the loser. He is exploited in the name of caste, community and religion by politicians who treat him as no better than part of a vote bank. Religious leaders have their own axe to grind. They spread superstition and witchcraft to keep people in bondage. The writer's heart bleeds for the poor, suffering people that form the bulk in this society.

Chapter 3

Tales from Firozsha Baag
An Ethnic Island

All art is mimetic, so said Aristotle. Rohinton Mistry's oeuvre is truly representational. His first offering *Tales from Firozsha Baag* describes a Parsi neighbourhood. The stress is not on action that could be essential for any conventional collection of stories, rather it is on the slow-but-real enough pace of life within the precincts of this ethnic island. The *Tales* sets the tone in such a manner that it can easily be considered a standard by which other works can be measured. Except for the story 'Squatters' in which Mistry gives free rein to his fancy, the anthology presents a perfect example of realistic portrayal of life.

The Parsi neighbourhood of the Firozsha Baag is housed in a triple-story complex consisting of blocks A, B and C. The families, whose tales are told, inhabit houses in different blocks but not all the residents find mention for obvious reasons. At the ground floor of Block A lives an old couple—Rustomji with his wife Mehroo. The first story 'Auspicious Occasion' is a snapshot of their life. Nariman Hansotia is his neighbour and he is immensely popular with the youngsters of the Baag as he relates stories to them. The story 'Squatters' shows Nariman as a storyteller. On the second floor lives a Parsi priest or Dustoorji. On the third floor lives the family of Viraf, a boy whose name occurs in the story 'Of White Hairs and Cricket.'

In B Block lives the only Muslim tenant with his Muslim servant. The eccentric old woman Khorshedbai lives with her husband Ardesar as paying guests of Boman and Kashmira, a young couple, much harassed by their tenants, who, it appears, are ironically referred to as guests. Jaykaylee, a maid and the narrator of the story 'The Ghost of Firozsha Baag' works here with a couple referred to as *bai-seth* by her. In C Block, the Boyce family lives on the ground floor. Kersi and Percy are the young boys belonging to this family. Kersi is the narrator of quite a few stories, viz., 'Of White Hairs and Cricket,' 'Lend me Your Light' and 'Swimming Lessons.' On the first floor of Block C, we find Najamai as well as Tehmina, both widows, living in close vicinity. Again, on the third floor of this block lives Dr. Mody, Principal of a veterinary college. His son Pesi or Peshotan earns notoriety for being a bully. The Mody family's neighbours are the Bulsaras of the story 'Exercisers.' It is in C Block that the lady Daulat who lost her husband Minochar lives. She is the protagonist of the story 'Condolence Visit.'

Apart from the characters broadly hinted at here are a number of minor characters also. Overall, this residential complex had "a surfeit of low-paid bank clerks and bookkeepers." (80) The narrative is concentric in nature so that whereas we have side roles for a neighbour in one story, in another he or she becomes the central character. Thus, in the story 'One Sunday,' Kersi and Percy are shown as teenagers who are sent out to catch Francis but in the last story, 'Lend me Your Light,' Kersi is shown as a budding writer settled in Canada.

Mistry's *Tales from Firozsha Baag* is primarily a study in human relationships. Although the community living within the precincts of the building is Parsi, yet this fact does not deprive the stories of their universal character. Besides, there are also inter-faith and inter-race dealings. We see the Parsis interacting with the Muslim neighbours, although with hesitation as the story 'The Paying Guest' shows. Christian characters like Francis of the story 'One Sunday' does not occupy the social status enjoyed by the Parsis. He is only a poor handyman, a subaltern. So, while the dealings with the Muslim gentleman do not start because of the historical memory, those with the Christian subaltern get bogged down due to the usual prejudices against the poor people. In place of Francis, we could have had any other Indian with similar results.

Within the Parsi community of the Firozsha Baag, we also find differences in terms of sex, age, economic status etc. While the youngsters like Percy, Jehangir, Kersi and Peshi remind us of any Indian neighbourhood, there is no bar to friendship between Dr. Mody and Jehangir. This is a mature person's way of making amends for the inanities of his son Peshi towards Jehangir. Another character striking the best of rapport across this generation gap is Nariman, who relates stories to the cricket-playing children of the block.

There are the Parsis like Jamshed who behave like the brown sahibs and hate India as well as things Indian. They can distance themselves from their kith and kin here without any pricks of conscience whatsoever. But there are also Parsis like Percy, who forget their individuality and dedicate their lives to the service of fellow Indians. Racial prejudices are too trivial to present obstacles to their higher minds.

The thing to be noted here is the remarkable ease with which Mistry delineates the complex relationships criss-crossing the large number of characters residing in the building. Except for the fantastic story about Sarosh ('Squatter'), we have a very realistic portrayal of the characters. Unless self-interest comes in the way, human beings, particularly those inhabiting this part of the world, get swayed by emotions. Emotions are more dominant in young people rather than the old ones. So, the young Kersi suffers himself in the humiliation of Francis and breaks his bat. Najamai, the old lady, does notice the urine at the back of the door but her reaction is devoid of sentiments. She matter-of-factly thinks about finding another handyman only! This genteel neighbourhood has its own bourgeois code of conduct. The middle class fetishes certain actions like seeing children move to western countries, particularly America and Canada. They must not mingle with the underdogs.

The sociologists view the family as the most important primary group in a society. It is responsible for the physical and mental growth, socialization and acculturation of the new as well as the existing members of a society. The *Tales* deals with different types of family structures. Starting with single individuals like Najamai, whose daughters have deserted her for foreign shores, we have aged couples like Rustomji-Mehroo as also young ones like Boman-Kashmira, with their old tenant Ardesar and his eccentric wife Khorshedbai. Apart from it, Daulat is shown as having been recently widowed. These are the stories of relationships which are under far greater strain in our times than they were at any other point of time in history and Mistry has the insight to grasp the complexity of evolving relationships in this collection.

The story 'The Collectors' presents a spoilt child Peshi or Peshotan, living with his parents Mrs. and Dr. Burjor Mody. The father is known for his social bent of mind. The name Peshotan is drawn from the Persian literature. It is the name of a noble general and lover of art but the Pesi of this story is a ruffian who brings bad name to his parents. Naturally, the parents are not proud of their only son whose additional qualification is rudely breaking wind in public. Concerned over the ill-treatment of a neighbourhood boy Jehangir Bulsara by his son, Dr. Mody invites the boy into his house and shares with him his personal collection of postal stamps. The story also has the psychological strain in that a class bully Eric D'Souza forces Jehangir into having homosexual relations with him right in the class. He also has the audacity to involve the boy in stealing stamps from the wayside vendors. This is his way of rewarding Jehangir for his docility, but soon the heist is discovered leading to much humiliation for Jehangir. It was Dr. Mody who had inspired Jehangir to collect stamps but when a certain Spanish stamp was found missing from the vet's collection, the needle of suspicion pointed to the boy only. Jehangir did not defend himself; he had been psychologically affected and so considered himself at fault.

The story 'One Sunday' opens with the news of Najamai, a middle-aged widow, planning to proceed to her sister's house in Bandra to spend the Sunday there. Her own house in the Baag is left to the care of the neighbours. Not that they would stand guard over her apartment, but that they would use her refrigerator in her absence (because they themselves do not own one) and these visits on purpose would ensure safety of Najamai's house. As Rohinton Mistry is based in Canada, it appears he has the western reader in his mind when he makes note of even the petty exchanges taking place in this genteel neighbourhood. The fact that Tehmina takes ice from Najamai's fridge and the Boyces keep beef in it regularly without suffering any pricks of conscience should definitely be of interest to the foreign readers. Of course, they reciprocate the gesture in their own ways. The Boyces let their newspaper be read by Najamai in the evening and their children Percy and Kersi are at the disposal of Najamai for the purpose of purging her house of rats. The boys use their bats for the purpose. The beef-eating by the Parsis is not due to taste entirely. Beef is, in fact, cheaper than mutton and the Parsis residing in the Baag are drawn to it due to the economic factor also.

On the particular Sunday, whose tale is told by Mistry, Tehmina could not close the door to Najamai's house properly as she suffered from cataract. She sought the assistance of Francis, the odd-job man for the entire neighbourhood, who had been lurking around for some work because he had been out of money and had not had food for two days. He was a Christian, as the name shows, but again it would be wrong to think all Christians are well-off just as it is untrue of the Parsis. Evidently, he did not lock the door properly and later in the evening, sensing the opportunity, slipped into the apartment with the intent to eat something or maybe steal something. At around ten when Najamai returned to the Baag, Francis was inside her apartment. On the way, she borrowed newspaper from Silloo Boyce as she did it regularly. While preparing to retire for the night, she spotted Francis behind the kitchen door and immediately shouted for help. Sillo Boyce and other neighbours rushed in. Meanwhile, Francis ran towards the Tar Gully. Now, Percy and Kersi were sent to fetch Francis.

The Tar Gully is shown as the abode of the subaltern. When the Boyce boys were spotted there by the natives—the 'ghatis,' they made fun of the boys carrying cricket bats at night. When the boys neared Francis, others also came to know of Francis's black deed and pounced on him. Even though the Tar Gully residents had the same socio-economic status which Francis had, yet they could not condone his lapse. Francis was beaten black and blue and spat upon with such vehemence that it made the boys feel sick. After he was brought back, the poor fellow was subjected to a fresh round of thrashing before being let off.

Back in her apartment, Najamai spotted urine at the back of the door and had a mixed feeling of anger and pity for Francis who was well-known in the community and had now ostensibly lost the trust. Kersi felt sorry for having gone after Francis with the bat. He could not openly sympathize with the Christian subaltern but had feeling of remorse later. As a reaction, he unwound the cord round its handle and broke it. The pent-up emotions of the young boy were thus released. Mistry rightly chooses a tender-hearted youngster to convey his humanist standpoint, for the grown-ups have lost the sensitivity.

Thinking about the ways to tackle different problems of the community should be the first priority with the leadership of the community. But it appears the community lacks effective leadership in this area. In post-independence India, most of the Parsis have been concerned with writing individual success stories in industry, services, professions, arts, literature etc. The Parsi Panchayat, on which the mantle to take action for the welfare of the community fell, has hardly come up to the expectations. Apart from marriage, there are several matters on which intra-community discussions and actions take place. One such area of common interest is the construction and maintenance of exclusive Parsi apartment blocks, particularly in Mumbai. Mistry's description of such buildings in the *Tales* reveals considerable dissatisfaction among the residents.

In the very first story 'Auspicious Occasion,' Rustomji is peeved over the refusal of the managing committee of the Parsi building to undertake repair work in the flats. When his wife suggests that they should hire their own plumber, Rustomji bursts out: "I will not spend one paisa of my hard-earned earnings! Those scoundrels sitting with piles of trust money hidden under their arses should pay for it!" (5). There ensued a period of one-upmanship and brinkmanship but the trustees would not budge. The tenants started looking after their own flats but "to this day Rustomji stubbornly held out, calling his neighbours fools for making things easy for the trustees instead of suffering the discomfort of peeling walls till the scoundrels capitulated" (6).

The neighbourly relations as portrayed in the *Tales* are not ideal, but the portrayal is certainly realistic. In the Indian situation, it is not uncommon to find jealous neighbours who would not be comfortable with a prosperous family. Rustomji, having proved his miserliness in the matter of spending money on the upkeep of society flat leased out to him, is not happy with Nariman Hansotia because he led others in not toeing Rustomji's line of action. Through Nariman's efforts, they agreed to pool in some money and hire a contractor to paint the exterior of A Block. The result was that Nariman refused point-blank to contribute for this cause, inviting the appellation 'curmudgeon' for himself. Mistry relishes the title he has chosen for his character thus: "Out of this exchange had grown an appended name: Rustomji-the-curmudgeon, and it had spread through Firozsha Baag, enjoying long life and considerable success."

Not to be cowed down still, Nariman persuaded the neighbours to go ahead with the paint work on self-help basis and leave Rustomji's flat. But when the work was over and Nariman waited for his rival's discomfiture over one begrimed piece studded in the overall freshly painted scenario, this is what Rustomji said of it, "Mr. Hansotia bought a new suit, and it has a patch on one knee." (6) The game of neighbourly jealousy and outwitting continues but surely this is not far from reality.

The story 'Of White Hairs and Cricket' is connected to the history of Parsis during the British times. Race and religion have played an important role in the game of cricket in colonial India. Clubs and Gymkhanas were created during that period and players in white played cricket. Indians were their subjects, so they were not considered fit for cricket. Bombay (now Mumbai) was the place where cricket was played by Indians first of all. The Parsis (also called Zoroastrians) took to this game as a community. They had at that time a small population, but on account of their talent for business, they came in contact with the British and adopted their ways.

Over the period, they developed closeness with the British and became quite westernised. The Parsis founded in1848 in Bombay the first Indian cricket club which was called The Oriental Cricket Club. Several other clubs were also founded by the Parsis. Leading Parsi businessmen like the Tatas and the Wadias sponsored these clubs. The white cricket clubs did not extend any help to these Parsi clubs. There is a record of a quarrel between Bombay Gymkhana, which was a club of the 'whites' (Europeans) and the Parsis over the use of a public park. The ponies used by the whites for playing polo dug up the surface of the park. So, it was left unfit for use by the Parsis. The administration naturally supported the white club. Finally, the Parsis decided to build their own gymkhana for playing cricket. A Parsi cricket team also defeated the Bombay Gymkhana team in 1889. After the success of the Parsi Gymkhana, several other Indian groups set up clubs on the basis of religious identity.

The story 'Of White Hairs and Cricket' mentions in some details the cricket-fixation of the teenagers of the Firozsha Baag:

> Cricket on Sunday mornings became a regular event for the boys in Firozsha Baag. Between us we almost had a complete kit; all that was missing was a pair of bails, and wicket keeping gloves. Daddy took anyone who wanted to play to the Marine Drive maidaan, and organized us into teams, captaining one team himself. We went early, before the sun got too hot and the maidaan overcrowded. (116-17)

The narrator's father felt indisposed one day and after that they shifted the activity to the compound of the Baag, though it had to be abandoned as it led to some ludicrous situation: "Its flag-stoned surface would not accept the points of stumps, and we chalked three white lines on the compound's black stone wall. But the compound was too cramped for cricket. Besides, the un-even ground made the ball bounce and rear erratically. After a few shattered panes of glass and several complaints from neighbours, the games ceased." (117)

The western style of living is not only reflected in their formal dress worn at the workplace by men and women, it is also to be found in the eating habits. Beef-eating is a taboo for the Hindus but the Parsis like it just as the English people do. In the story 'One Sunday,' the Boyce family keeps its weekly supply of beef in Najamai's refrigerator. Tehmina, a female character of this very story, is addicted to scotch and soda. Dina Shroff's wedding in *A Fine Balance* is celebrated with drinks and the women also drink. This is a western tradition which is approved for Parsi marriages. With the passage of time, however, in urban India at least, women belonging to the upper income bracket have also started drinking.

The western inclination of the Parsis is also revealed in their bias for the fair colour of body. This colour prejudice is reflected when the children of the story 'The Ghost of Firozsha Baag' call out 'Blackie, blackie,' the moment they spot Jaykaylee. She is aware of this tendency of the Parsis as is ap-parent from her remark: "Parsis prefer Mangalorean Catholics, they have light skin colour. For themselves also Parsis like light skin and when Parsi baby is born that is the first and most important thing. If it is fair they say, O how nice light skin just like parents. But if it is dark skin they say, *arre* what is this *ayah no chhokro*, ayah's child" (46). It is interesting to see colour being used as a tool by one subaltern group against the descendants of a former master race, since in the Goan maid's veins ran partially the blood of the Portuguese masters and Af-rican slaves (Bharucha 83-84). In the story 'One Sunday,' the new generation of Parsis is brought in to underline its attitude to the subaltern Francis. The young generation does not share the viewpoint of the older generation in any society. Kersi, though a part of the brigade that catches the 'thief' Francis and teaches him a lesson, does have pangs of remorse in which he cracks the handle of the cricket bat.

The Parsis have maintained their separate identity on the basis of their religion and are, therefore, sensitive about their faith. Mistry misses no opportunity to dwell on the description of religious practices and rituals. The story 'Auspicious Occasion' revolves around the *Behram roje* or the Parsi new year. For Rustomji, the day has special significance because on this day his *navjote* ceremony was performed when he was only seven year old. He wears a gleaming white *dugli* and also puts on his *pheytoe* (cap) to follow his wife to the *agyaree* or the fire temple, though the plan misfires due to the misdemeanour of a fellow bus passenger, another aspect of social life in India. The use of such words in their original form in the book lends an authentic touch to this realistic portrayal. It must be noted here that despite his penchant for the details of religious ceremonies, Mistry has reservations about many aspects. In this story, as in most of his novels, the *dustoorji* or the priest is mocked at. Rustomji remarks about *dustoor* Dhunjisha:

> Loves to touch and feel women, the old goat—the younger and fleshier, the more fun he has hugging and squeezing them. But this was not all. Rustomji swore that Dhunjisha and his ilk had been known to exchange lewd remarks between lines of prayer, to slip them in amidst scripture recitals, especially on days of ceremony when sleek nubile women in their colourful finery attended in large numbers. The oft-repeated Ashem Vahoo was his favourite example:
>
> Ashem Vahoo,
> See the tits on that chickie-boo. (13-14)

However, the Parsi community presents a paradox in that even though it lays claim to being an educationally advanced group, there is no dearth of people wedded to superstitions. A dimension of this blind faith is seen in the form of belief in ghosts in the story 'The Ghost of Firozsha Baag.' The story is narrated in first person mode by a Goan Christian maid called Jaykaylee, who works in the household of a Parsi couple referred to as the *seth* and *bai*. Her real name was Jacqueline but the name was distorted through incorrect pronunciation by the people. While the local Hindu servants referred to as 'ghatis' and female servants called 'Gangas' also worked for the Parsis, the latter as proud inheritors of the colonial legacy deemed it a matter of prestige to employ Goan Christian maids for their children. As Jaykaylee muses, "they thought they were like British only, ruling India, side by side." (46) Since the Goan Christians were fluent in English, they were in good demand. Another factor to be noted here is that the lighter-skinned Mangalorese maids were preferred to the dark-skinned Goan ones. This fascination for English language and fair colour has been noted by Mistry in his novels also.

This Jaykaylee had been with the family ever since the *seth* was a toddler himself. The musings of the maid show her nostalgia about the period when she was young and energetic. Now, grinding chillies etc. for curries meant a lot of fatigue for her. There is an implicit sexual undercurrent in the description of the act of cooking and eating spiced curries and indeed the story takes it to a climax with the suggestive details of the company of the 'ghost.' It can also be seen as a fantastic ploy used by the maid to spice up her dull routine.

At first, the report of the maid Jaykaylee about having seen the ghost on Christmas night was ridiculed. She felt humiliated because the *seth* had been served by her since his childhood. The story went round and she became the butt of ridicule when urchins likened her to the ghost. Taking a cue from this, even the adolescent boys started teasing girls unnecessarily. Finally, the elders stepped in and stopped this 'bhoot game.' However, when her *bai* returned with the *seth* at the dead of night on the New year eve and mistook the maid's figure wrapped up in white and standing at the head of the staircase for a ghost, the rumour got a boost and from individual schizophrenic act, it became a group fixation in no time so much so that even prayers were arranged to rid the building of the ghost. Now that both the women testified to the presence of the ghost, an exorcist was also called in and his services availed.

There is intentional obfuscation here regarding the identity of the 'ghost' who is hinted at as Pesi, the wayward son of the Modis. The ghost reminds her of her boyfriend of youth whose name was Catejan. She eats fish on Friday and the bhoot comes only that day. She confesses before the priest, who gives her three Hail Marys and says eating fish is fine. After that the ghost does not bother her, she keeps waiting for the ghost though. It is left to the imagination of the reader to decide if the maid liked the physical proximity of the boy-ghost or feared it.

References such as these to the superstitions are found aplenty in the *Tales from Firozsha Baag*. In the 'Condolence Visit,' there is reference to Minocher accusing his wife Daulat when she resists eating oxtail. It is for her susceptibilities that he himself also abstains from it. This kind of superstition apart, we see sometimes this tendency transmuted into the realm of thinking about life itself. Thus, determinism or too much faith in destiny can also be treated as an offshoot of superstition. Perhaps it is this kind of thinking that seems to have guided Mistry in holding fate responsible for the betal nut juice spewed on Rustomji's *dugli* on the auspicious occasion of *Behram roje*: "But unbeknown to Rustomji, on the upper deck sat fate in the form of a mouth chewing tobacco and betel nut, a mouth with a surfeit of juice and aching jaws crying for relief. And when the bus halted at Marine Lines, fate leaned out of the window to release a generous quantity of sticky, viscous, dark red stuff." (17)

Thus, in day-to-day life, numerous occasions display the streak of superstition. In the story 'Of White Hairs and Cricket,' the narrator, a young boy, is called upon every Sunday to pick out the white hairs of his father but his grandmother considers this as an inauspicious activity and castigates the father for indulging in 'duleendar' things like this. (109). Again, a sweeper-ess crossing Tehmina's path invites a volley of curses. Her morning routine is described in a very interesting manner by Mistry:

> And the old spinster Tehmina, still waiting for her cataracts to ripen, would be saying her prayers facing the rising sun, with her duster-coat hoisted up and slung over the left shoulder, her yellowing petticoat revealed, to untie and tie her shoulder, her thick rope like Kusti around the waist; and the *kuchrawalli* would be sweeping the compound, making her rounds from door to door with broom and basket, collecting yesterday's garbage. If she happened to cross Tehmina's line of vision, all the boys were sure to have a fine time, because Tehmina, though blurry with cataract, would recognize the *kuchrawalli* and let loose at her with a stream of curses fouler than any filth in the garbage basket, for committing the unspeakable crime of passing in front of her, thereby polluting her prayers and vitiating their efficacy. (114)

Rohinton Mistry has a strange obsession with taking copious notes of various ceremonies of his community. The reader's knowledge of the Parsi customs is truly enhanced by the writer. Starting with the story 'Auspicious Occasion,' we are introduced to the food preferences of the Parsi community. Mehroo had cooked *dhandar-paatyo* and *Sali-boti* that morning, but in other stories there are repeated references to *dhansaak* which makes it amply clear that this must be the most popular dish. The dress code for such special occasions like the Parsi new year prescribes a *dugli* besides the usual shirt and trousers. *Kusti*, which is worn by every Parsi, is also woven at home. This job is done by Mamaiji (grandmother) in the story 'Of White Hairs and Cricket.' One also notes the peculiar words of salutation used by the Parsis: the narrator on accosting the doctor greets him with the words "Sahibji, doctor."

The story 'Condolence Visit' also meticulously details the rites and ceremonies connected with death. Daulat Mirza, the protagonist of this story, has recently lost her husband Minocher. As is normal on such occasions, her neighbours, relatives and acquaintances pour in to express their grief. Sarosh, also known as Sid, is her nephew and he has flown in from Canada for the purpose. He is the same Sid about whom a story 'Squatter' is included in this collection. He is reported to have brought a gift of a tape recorder earlier. At that time Minocher was ill and Daulat had refused to accept the gift saying, "Poor Minocher sick in bed and I listen to music? Never" (60). In a way, this morose attitude prefigured the greater tragedy lying in store for Minocher.

As is the practice among the Parsis, the visits in honour of the dead start after the tenth day of the demise of a person. This day is called the 'dusmoo.' People stream in repeating usual platitudes. Daulat becomes sick of pulling a long face again and again. But it is a solemn occasion and she has to undergo the trauma. Mistry finds an opportunity to relieve the gloomy atmosphere. People ask usual questions about the deceased. All this makes Daulat wish she had the tape recorder with her so that she would have played the taped answer in response to the routine queries of the mourners. Her neighbour Najamai rises to the occasion and brings in chairs and glasses for the growing number of visitors. The Parsis are no exception to the common courtesy seen in Indian society. People in the vicinity try their utmost to make the bereaved person comfortable. But there is the flip side also: Najamai is also a source of irritation to Daulat because of her naivete. Her unsolicited advice about the lamp lit in Minocher's room is not liked by Daulat. Najamai says that the lamp ought to be put out on the fourth day when the *charam* ceremony is held, because that would help the soul to travel to the next world. In case the lamp is not extinguished, the soul would be in the doldrums, so to say, as it would be attracted to two different places: here and the Next World. As it was, Daulat liked the lamp burning. It provided her some strange type of comfort. She shuts the door finally so that the lamp is not seen by Najamai.

A feature associated with the dead or the dying is the use of the perfume called 'eau de cologne' on the forehead. This is done to relieve the sick-room of the foul smells. In case of the dead, a little perfume is still sprinkled around the body. This is quite common among the Parsi community. A junior priest has the duty to keep the bottle of perfume with him. The richer the Parsi, the costlier is the variety of eau de cologne used by him for his near and dear ones. Parsi writers tell us that the community's western bent of mind necessitated the import of perfume from foreign countries.

One of the customs among the Parsis that Mistry dwells on is the wearing of a special type of headgear called 'pugree.' This is a necessary part of dress on festive occasions. In the story 'Condolence Visit,' the pugree of the dead man becomes the bone of contention. It was a tall black hat that the Parsi men wore on occasions like wedding. Not many Parsi boys wear such purgree now and due to plummeting demand, such splendid pugrees are not commonly available. Daulat had advertised in the local Parsi newspaper *Jam-e-Jamshed* that the pugree would be given to the person who really understood its importance and needed it. A person contacted Daulat and was expected to come to collect the pugree.

It so happened that the youngman arrived at this very moment. When Najamai and another relative Moti came to know of the purpose of his visit, they seemed horrified beyond limit. They would have none of it so soon after the death of the wearer of the pugree. But Daulat did not buckle and gave the pugree to the youngman without any payment. Later, she put off the lamp also. The story shows the strong-minded Daulat steadfast in her love for her beloved husband but not affected in the least by the superstitious views of the people around her. Mistry has thus tried to put a question mark on the petty and meaningless details associated with Parsi customs. Love and affection for our dear ones cannot be judged by anybody outside our own selves, for these are the matters of heart and soul and no measure has been devised to weigh their worth.

Other social issues that Mistry touches upon include the intractable tenant-landlord problem. As is widely known, in case of any dispute between the two parties, the law is on the side of the tenant. The story 'The Paying Guests' highlights this injustice when Mr. Karani tells Boman that "it was easier to get rid of a poisonous *kaankhajuro* which had crawled through your ear and nibbled its way to your brain than to evict a paying guest who had been allowed into your flat." (127) How the eccentric old lady Khorshedbai torments her young and gentle landlord and landlady at a time when they are expecting their first child and need the room let out to the 'paying guests' for their personal use! Mr. Karani's words are a poignant reminder to Boman: "To get rid of that problem there is no remedy except death." (131) Though Boman institutes legal proceedings against his tenants, he feels hamstrung because no neighbour or relative is ready to testify in the court because of the hassles involved in litigation. While the usually drawn-out legal battles going on for years and years with no avail to the aggrieved party are a common knowledge, the episode also reflects badly on the selfish nature of the Parsis of our times. Boman is sure that his only Muslim neighbour would testify but then out-group prejudice comes in the way.

Ultimately, it is the monstrosity of Khorshedbai's depraved mind which manifests itself when she puts the infant in the cage that the conscience of the neighbours is aroused and they consent to testify against the woman though that is no longer needed. The Parsi community, like any elite group, shies away from sacrificing personal comfort and smugness to take up the difficult path of good neighbourliness. But still there are limits to it and the deeply ingrained sense of justice and fair play cries for compliance when things cross a certain limit. Social protest and the consequent desire for change stem from such a situation.

The story 'Auspicious Occasion' also gives details of the relationship between the Parsi community and other communities. Mehroo goes to the fire temple to celebrate the *roje*, Rustomji is supposed to follow her. There are details of rituals performed on this occasion like decorating main entrance doors with fragrant flowers and the thresholds with coloured designs. Special dishes are cooked on this occasion and incense sticks lit in home. Rustomji travels by bus to reach the fire temple or the *agiary*, as it is referred to by the Parsis. As he alights from the bus, a fellow releases tobacco juice on his white *dugli*. He is surrounded by the local people, who enjoy his discomfiture. There are some who sympathize wit! him in their own style as is clear from the remark, "Bawaji got pan-pichkari right on his white *dugli*" (17). Rustomji is irritated and calls them "sisterfucking *ghatis*." This arouses spirit of vengeance through the non-Parsi crowd. Fortunately, Rustomji has presence of mind and he makes fun of himself by taking out dentures saying "*Arre* please *yaar*, why harass an old man. . . . Look, such an old man, no teeth even." (18) He is handed over a newspaper by one to wrap his dugli in and he returns home. This is not an endearing picture of the relationship obtaining between the Parsi community and others in the Indian society, but the event is quite realistically and convincingly portrayed. Mistry means to underline here the need for different communities, more so in case of a minority, to have self-restraint.

The story 'Auspicious Occasion' now takes the reader to the fire-temple where all is not well. The *dustoorji* or the priest of the temple is reported to have been killed by the *chasniwalla* or the assistant, who was trying to steal something and was spotted by *dustoorji*. Mehroo is shocked to learn of the development, tries to find her husband in the melee and having failed in the attempt, returns home. Here she finds Rustomji's *dugli* splashed red and taking the betel juice for blood, screams, "*Dustoor* Dhunjisha's *dugli*! But . . . but . . . how did you—?" Reality is explained now but the nervousness caused by the incident must be marked. For the Parsis, the murder of the *Dustoor* by a co-religionist indicates failure of the safety mechanism of the community. The significance of this incident can be gauged from the fact that the number of Parsis is already on the decline.

The story 'Exercisers' revolves around the story of the boy Jehangir who was earlier introduced to the reader in the story 'The Collectors' as a shy, studious boy, honed into a stamp collector by Dr. Modi. The story also depicts the impact of the majority culture on a minority existing as an island in an ocean. The

Balsaras visit Bhagwan Baba, ostensibly a Hindu holy man as the name suggests, along with their college-going son Jehangir. The purpose of the visit is to wean the son away from a girl to whom he has lately taken fancy. The Bulsaras think the girl is shrewd enough to be trying to ensnare their son because he is destined to go to America. The western influence on the Parsis comes in clash with the growing influence of the majority community even in this over-patronizing attitude towards the child.

In the last two decades, the lure of the lucre has attracted many an Indian to foreign shores, particularly of America. The Parsis have also come under the sway of this phenomenon. Those willing to migrate have mostly gone to Canada. This fact finds adequate coverage in the *Tales*. Najamai's daughters Dolly and Vera have gone abroad leaving their widowed mother behind. Similarly, Karsi, on coming of age, is almost forced to go abroad by voxpop of the Parsi neighbourhood. It is not that the young Parsis are devoid of any feelings of attachment. Karsi's reflection is full of gaps and therefore self-revealing: "Half jokingly, I saw myself as someone out of a Greek tragedy, guilty of the sin of hubris for seeking emigration out of the land of my birth, and paying the price in burnt-out eyes: I, Tiresias, blind and throbbing between two lives, the one in Bombay and the one to come in Toronto" (180). This identity confusion among the young Parsis has become another notable social phenomenon.

As discussed earlier, the America or Canada-fixation is almost central to the aspirations of the majority of Parsis. If the story 'Squatter' deals with Sid's maladjustment in Canada, the last story in the anthology 'Lend Me Your Light' probes the possibilities of peace, not just of body and mind but deep in one's soul in the midst of sordid Indian reality. In this story, India-basher Jamshed is pitted against an idealist Percy, who is considered a failure by the Parsis because he finds his authentic being in serving the rural poor in India against heavy odds and at great risk to his own life. It is, once again, as in the story 'The Paying Guest,' the question of the level of personal perception and commitment that enables one to take on the deluge of social opposition and introduce gradual transformation of social outlook. Through the character of Percy, Mistry holds an ideal before his community and wants his community to build bridges with the society at large though it might entail inconvenience and demand sacrifices.

Migration to the west is causing concern because the community already faces the problem of dwindling numbers in India. An estimate of their total population suggests the number of one lakh Parsis, out of whom some 60,000 are in India alone. Mistry is concerned about this trend. An important factor that has led to decelerated growth of the community is the growing tendency of young men and women to marry late in life. Material success has become more important in their eyes than the emotional succour that the partners in marriage look for. That Mistry is most concerned about this situation can be gauged from the fact that he takes up this problem in each one of his works. In the *Tales*, the protagonist of 'Swimming Lessons' muses: "The Parsi community has the highest divorce rate in India. It also claims to be the most westernized community in India. Which is the result of the other?" (230) Mistry is also not happy about the state of health of the Parsis. Stereotypes of Parsees are painted as ageing or aged people suffering from one disease or the other. The persona referred to above also comments: "We are the chosen people where osteoporosis is concerned." (230)

Class consciousness or elitism as a socio-psychological trait among the Parsis also comes in for comment by Mistry. History is witness to the fact that the Parsis enjoyed enviable position during the British rule over India. The English, understandably, cultivated the Parsis because they were well-educated, had no political aspirations and were not native to the soil. Charges of collusion with the British were commonly levelled against them despite the fact that the freedom struggle was duly contributed to by some great Parsi figures. After the attainment of independence, a large section of the Parsis felt like having lost out on power. This feeling continued to grow and reached a stage of alienation from the native Indians. Their ever-reducing number added to the sense of insecurity. Under the circumstances, it was natural for them to be wary of the majority which threatened to swamp them. It is common observation that a community views the other community with some kind of suspicion. This is a tribal instinct that has travelled down to our times since times immemorial. In case of the Parsis, who are threatened with dwindling numbers and the consequent sense of insecurity, the bias against the majority community surrounding them has got to be more acute. The colonial hangover that has got diluted to aristocratic exclusivist mindset also adds extra flavour to it.

Their class prejudice is also reflected in the catch-words like *ghatans* or *ghatis* used for the residents of coastal areas (Western Ghat) or even for all other Indians and is indicative of their out-group phobia. Similarly, all Hindu maids are *gangas* for them. The story 'Auspicious Occasion' presents a thesis of sorts on the '*gangas.*' Rustomji explains the psychology of the maids thus: "If a particular day is important, never let the *ganga* know, pretend everything is normal. And never, never ask her to come earlier than usual, for she will deliberately come late" (8). In the cloistered settlements of Parsis, the maids are the only natives to come in contact with them on daily basis. This kind of interaction does lead to some degree of satisfaction after having lost the pre-colonial clout with the ruling class.

This prejudice against the *ghatis* is ingrained at an early age in the Parsis. The protagonist of 'Lend Me Your Light' remembers his college days when he inhered this complex but rose above it as is evident from the following peep in his mind: "With much shame I remember this word *ghati*. A suppurating sore of a word, oozing the stench of bigotry. It consigned a whole race to the mute roles of coolies and menials, forever unredeemable" (176). This character Percy shows the reformist side of Mistry in that he ultimately chooses to cast his lot with these very *ghatis*: he works for the uplift of the downtrodden living in remote villages. While doing this, he courts real danger to his own self while his ideologue comrade is killed by the agents of vested interests desiring status quo. On the one hand, this incident shows the class consciousness that Mistry as a sociologist evinces, on the other it reveals Mistry's preference for voluntarism that is Gandhian in character. This shade of Mistry's thinking is verified by the following observation of his character regarding the female native workers: "I was never sure why some people called them *ghatons* and others, *gungas*. I supposed the latter was intended to placate—the collective conferment of the name of India's sacred river balanced the occasions of harshness and ill-treatment" (177). If the minority community has coined words for the majority community, how can the latter lag behind? So, people from the majority community call the Parsis 'Bawaji,' the 'ji' suffix mercifully serves as an honorific.

Although Mistry has not yet indulged in politician bashing, a reference here and there is surely found hinting at the disapproval of the Machiavellian creatures. Thus, Late Prime Minister Indira Gandhi's Garibi Hatao programme launched during the emergency does find a brief mention in the story 'The Collectors': "The Bombay police, in a misinterpretation of the nation's mandate: garibi hatao—eradicate poverty, conducted periodic round ups of pavement dwellers, sweeping into their vans beggar and street vendors, cripple and alcoholics, the homeless and the hungry, and dumped them somewhere outside the city limits; when the human detritus made its way back into the city, another clean-up was scheduled." (98). Two vendors *Patla* and *Jhaaria* fall victim to this 'poverty eradication' drive.

There are stories in which Mistry focuses on the relationship of the Indian Parsis with the outside world. In his stories 'Squatter' and 'Swimming Lessons,' Mistry widens his area of sociological study to include the Parsi diaspora in Canada. It gives him an opportunity to dwell upon the equation evolving between this community and the Canadians. As is natural under the circumstances, problems of all sorts do come up and individuals, for those who immigrate to Canada are loners and even otherwise the western society being highly individualistic one, have to depend upon their own resources to cope with the situation. This, quite often, gives rise to funny situations as, for example, in 'Squatter.'

The protagonist of the story is Sarosh or Sid who has already been introduced to the reader as Daulat's nephew in the story 'Condolence Visit.' The story is related by Nariman Hansotia to the children of the Firozsha Baag in the orature tradition of story telling. Prior to this, he has also related the story of a great Parsi cricketer and hunter Savukshaw. According to the renowned critic Nilufer Bharucha, "The shame and ignominy of the contemporary Parsi immigrant to the West is thus off-set by the swashbuckling Parsi of yore." (103). The story of the immigrant Sid presents a contrast because he has failed to finetune his life-style to the demand of the Canadian situation unlike Savukshaw's adaptability to the English game of cricket. So, in Mistry's repertoire, we have perfect matches co-existing with mismatches, something that should make his stories so realistic but for the element of hyperbole that stands out in 'Squatter.'

Even after ten years of stay in Canada, Sid is far from being a happy man, the reason being his inability to answer nature's call sitting in what is usually referred to as the English seat. Ten years is a long time indeed but more than that it puts the reader as well as the protagonist in mind of the promise that Sid had made to his parents and friends that if he could not acclimatize himself to the Canadian environment, he would return to India for ever. The problem each morning in the bathroom is a terse reminder to him of his failure and the attending promise. He would not try squatting on the seat like the westerners. The resulting scene as described by the writer has to be read to enjoy its comicality:

> The absence of feet below the stall door, the smell of faeces, the rustle of paper, glimpses caught through the narrow crack between the stall door and jamb—all these added up to only one thing: a foreign presence in the stall, not doing things in the conventional way. And if the one outside could receive the fetor of Sarosh's business wafting through the door, poor unhappy Sarosh too could

> detest something malodorous in the air: the presence of xenophobia and hostility. (156)

Sarosh's supervisor at work is an experienced hand and though Sid tries to avoid giving out the real reason for reporting late at work routinely, he can guess his problem that is normal in case of expatriates. Sid is suggested getting in touch with the Immigrant Aid Society. In the Indian Immigrant Aid Society, Mrs. Maha-Lepate recommends to him a certain Dr. No-Ilaz who is renowned for having treated several immigrants of the problem. The doctor with the funny name tells him about a funnier device called Crappus Non Interruptur or CNI that operates much like the remote garage door opener. But there is a hitch in that the remote could operate the bowels of any other person also, in case he was within the receiving range of the remote control device. That would make Sid also vulnerable to the remote control device held by any other person fitted with CNI. Sid can see the enormity of the problem and better sense prevails over him when he decides to migrate back to India rather than get himself fitted with the fantastic bowel-easing device.

He has four weeks left before he enplanes for India and in this period he tries hard to conform to the western pattern of passing stool but to no avail. He is late for work as usual and gets the pink slip before long. Mistry also takes pot-shots at Canada's pretensions of being a 'melting pot' and helping assimilation through its Multicultural Department. "If you ask me, mosaic and melting pot are both nonsense, and ethnic is a polite way of saying bloody foreigner." (160). Finally, when he is inside the plane which has started rolling on, he feels the urge to go to toilet. Without heeding the warning signals in the speeding aeroplane, he lunges for the bathroom and there for the first time in ten years is able to finish the job without squatting. Later, he grows philosophical and his musings are noted down by the writer in a mock-comic way:

> As the aircraft sped down the runway, Sarosh's first reaction was one of joy. The process of adaptation was complete. But later, he

> could not help wondering if success came before or after the ten-year limit had expired. And since he had already passed through the customs and security check, was he really an immigrant in every sense of the word at the moment of achievement? (166)

Since the plane was in motion, he could not have disembarked. He returns to a welcome party organized by friends and relatives though they are not able to understand as to what brought him back from that land of milk and honey. Sid is ill at ease here also because the old pattern of life is no longer available. One day, when the narrator Nariman Hansotia was driving past Marine Drive, he saw a 'forlorn and woebegone' Sid who does not wish to be called by that name for fear of being reminded of all travails back in Canada. He is disillusioned about ambitions hitched to foreign lands. It is here that he commands Nariman, in Shakespearean lingo, *a la* Othello:

> When you shall these unlucky deeds relate, speak of me as I am; nothing extenuate, nor set down aught in malice: tell them that in Toronto once there lived a Parsi boy as best as he could. Set you down this; and say, besides, that for some it was good and for some it was bad, but for me life in the land of milk and honey was just a pain in the posterior. (168)

The last story in this collection is titled 'Swimming Lessons' and it deals with the question of identity in the case of immigrant Indian Parsi Kersi. He along with his brother Percy was introduced to the reader in the story 'One Sunday.' Over the years, this sentimental boy, who broke his bat in a moment of repentance, has grown into a youngman and shifted to Canada as most aspiring Parsis have been doing. His is a different experience from Sid's total physical maladjustment. An element of sensuality has been thrown in. Beauty seems truly skin-deep as is connoted by the writer's remark about the sun-bathing beauties:

> They don't seem as attractive as they did from the kitchen window. The elevator arrives and I hold it open, inviting them in with what I think is a gallant flourish. Under the fluorescent glare in the elevator I see their wrinkled skin, aging hand, sagging bottoms, varicose

veins. The lustrous trick of sun and lotion and distance has ended. (233)

Lured by the prospect of getting within the touching distance of the women, Kersi joins swimming class. What he encounters there is open display of prejudice and acrimony against an Asian by other youngsters. As he enters the showers, three young boys, probably from the previous class emerge. "One of them holds his nose. The second begins to hum, under his breath: Paki, Paki, smell like curry. The third says to the first two: pretty soon all the water's going to taste of curry. They leave" (238). Racial prejudice against Parsis, whether in India or in Canada has not waned, only it has incorporated a slight difference: from Indian Parsi you are treated as an Asian there; from 'Bawaji' to 'Paki.'

It is poor consolation indeed to know that you would henceforth be discriminated against, not as a member of the small Parsi diaspora of a millennium-standing in India but of the large Asian presence that is around two-century old. But Mistry is right in sending the message that such prejudices are universal and unavoidable and therefore, those at the receiving end should keep their cool and carry on with their lives. There are other disappointments also in store for Kersi, the loss of a certain site of sexual significance, for which the costly bathing costume was purchased, being one. "Total losses: One fantasy plus thirty dollars." But what is more, "No watery rebirth. The swimming pool, like Chaupatty beach, has produced a stillbirth" (240). This failure of rebirth also allegorizes Kersi's failure to identify himself completely with the Canadians.

The story also takes in the reactions of Kersi's parents back in India. When a parcel is brought to his parents' house by the postman, his mother opens with excitement only to put hands on her face, for she has found something totally unexpected. The father takes over and notes that his son has turned writer and has sent them the story book written by him. The situation is bound to lead us to the surmise that Kersi is the alter ego of Mistry himself. The revelation is a pleasant surprise to Kersi's parents. Both of them read the stories. While the mother spots nostalgia for home, the father disagrees and says that all writers work in the same way using their memories and experiences. Mother throws the inevitable question, "how can you be sure that he is remembering because he is a writer, or whether he started to write because he is unhappy and thinks of his past, and wants to save it all by making stories of it." (243) Anyhow, Kersi's father is curious to read about his son's experiences abroad through these stories. He also wants Kersi to write stories that should concern the glory of ancient Parsis rather than the mundane life of immigrants in Canadian setting.

A parallel situation has also been created in the story in which an old Canadian and his son staying in the same apartment block drive away in cold snowy evening leaving the mother behind and Kersi's comment universalizes the experience, "And the further they go, the more they'll remember, they can take it from me." (247)

Chapter 4

Such a Long Journey: Understanding Human Nature

The pioneers of the Indian novel in English imbued their works with social realism. Stalwarts like Mulk Raj Anand, Raja Rao, R.K. Narayan, Bhabani Bhattacharya, et al analysed the social scenario and suggested remedies before the focus shifted to the individual psyche. Anand, for one, used Auguste Comte's sociology, illustrating how such social phenomena as untouchability or poverty in *Untouchable* and *Coolie* could be read in terms of the three stages of development—theological, metaphysical and positivistic. These three stages can be traced in history but they also co-exist, as for example, on a single day in the life of Bakha. In the long journey of the Indian novel written in English, sociological reading of Indian milieu lost its hold, giving place to newer readings. However, the old emphasis on sociology has returned, as for example, in Rohinton Mistry's *Such a Long Journey* which presents sociological perception of human nature. Before we take up this novel in detail, it would be fruitful to ascertain how the sociologists themselves view life.

Sociologists like Max Weber claim that "modern industrial society is characterized by 'rationalization and intellectualisation.' The world is no longer charged with mystery and magic; the supernatural has been banished from society" (Haralambos 484). On the other hand, we have scholars like Vilfredo Pareto who have shown the weak foundations of a rationalistic approach to society. He believes that human actions, for the most part, are guided not by logic or reason but by sentiments. Pareto represents one of the most distinguished intellectual currents in the European tradition. "That broad school of thought includes such diverse figures as Burke, Taine, Dostoyevsky, Burckhardt, Nietzsche and Spengler and stands in opposition to rationalism, liberalism, egalitarianism, Marxism, and all of the other offspring of Enlightenment doctrinaires" (Thornton). And it is this school of thought that seems to inspire Rohinton Mistry's work.

The first epigraph of the novel *Such a Long Journey* is a quotation from Firdausi's *Shahnama:*

> He assembled the aged priests and put questions to them concerning the kings who had once possessed the world. 'How did they,' he inquired, 'hold the world in the beginning, and why is it that it has been left to us in such a sorry state? And how was it that they were able to live free of care during the days of their heroic labours?'

Mistry has sought to underline here the fact that the early rulers held populace subjugated precisely because the masses lived by beliefs, at times, transcending their minds. One such dogmatic belief is called the theory of the divine right of kings. These early rulers exploited people's beliefs to the hilt, and as Firdausi learnt they left nothing worthwhile for the newer generations to fall back upon.

As the reader progresses through the novel, he finds that it is not only the people in the past who have been gullible at the hands of the Machiavellian rulers, our own lives are none too logically and scientifically lived. This novel is a story of a Parsee family. The head of the family Gustad, his wife Dilnavaz and their three children—Sohrab and Darius, both boys, and Roshan, a girl, live in Khodadad Building in Bombay. Their very ordinary middle class existence receives a jolt as they find themselves involved in a political scandal of international stature. This sensational event known as the Nagarwala scam is the one that rocked the Indira Gandhi government in the wake of the Bangladesh liberation struggle. The novel lays equal stress on the communal as well as the individual lives.

The novel has drawn heavily on that side of human life and activity which can be described as non-rational in the philosophical sense. Religious activity, for example, is one such facet which finds wide mention in the novel. The novel begins with the central character Gustad offering prayers to 'Ahura Mazda.' After finishing the prayer, as is the custom, Gustad cracks the kusti which action is symbolic of driving away the devil. But he does not resort to it merely as a religious gesture. In his mind are stored images of his childhood days when, with this action, he imagined driving away all sorts of ghosts and murderers. He continues to enjoy it with the same abandon even as a middle-aged man.

The reader is now treated to the happy news of Gustad's eldest son Sohrab's admission to the IIT. That is a dream-come-true situation for any middle-class youngster and his proud parents. As such, Gustad plans to celebrate it on the ninth birthday of his daughter Roshan but surprisingly Sohrab is not amused. Things go haywire on the party day with an unbridgeable gulf developing between the father and the son. Sohrab would just not listen to the suggestion of entering the portals of the hallowed precincts of IIT as he does not like the idea of getting separated from his friends, who ostensibly have taken up arts course in a college. All this appears so illogical and unreasonable to Gustad who blurts: "Throwing away his [Sohrab's] fortune without reason. What have I not done for him, tell me? I even threw myself in front of a car. Kicked him aside, saved his life, and got this to suffer all my life (slapping his hip). But that's what a father is for." (52)

His tiff with his son reminds us of the intransigence of his own father. 'One proud man's stubbornness' (101) is how Gustad referred to his father's soft corner for his dissolute uncle at the expense of Gustad's college fees. He never forgave his weak father for his 'effeminacy' and decided to grow strong as a rock. Now, that rock-like strength was being put to test by his own son who found him stubborn in wishing him to join IIT. Anyone would dub Sohrab's action as non-rational because it means honouring his emotional links with his buddies but Gustad also cannot be called a rationalist because it is his son who has to study and ultimately shape his life according to his own interests. The point Mistry makes is that our wishes propped by beliefs and sentiments, are not necessarily realized because there is no logical connection between what we wish and what happens.

Mistry, through this fiasco of the central wish, underlines his views about human nature which for all its evolution is still steeped in non-logical ways of thinking and acting. Mistry was not the first to present this sociological perception of human nature. I.A. Richards, in his essay 'Pseudo-statements' observes that most of our attitudes are determined by emotive responses rather than by scientific views. Poets are known for making pseudo statements such as the existence of God, of immortality, of freedom but such beliefs do serve some social purpose, when it comes to organizing society around rituals and ceremonies, around common beliefs and shared sentiments. Still, on the whole, these non-logical actions have also been exploited by those who are able to free themselves from these sentiments.

In the midst of the father-son stand-off, it is Dilnavaz, Sohrab's mother, who suffers. The special chicken dish is hardly consumed with six out of nine pieces remaining in the pot. Sohrab's uttering a volley of audacious words right in the face of his father appears like so much blasphemy to his mother. This gulf, most unfortunately, goes on widening and at one point of time, Sohrab walks out on his father and his family. This is indeed shocking. As a mother, Dilnavaz's utmost concern is to see her son reconciled to his father and the family re-united. She cannot think of any reasoned solution to this malady and falls for the utterly irrational and superstitious counsel of her neighbour Miss Kutpitia (which in Gujarati means 'the quarrelsome one'), an elderly and freakish spinster who acts as the community advisor of queer medicines, prescribing lemons and chillies to win over the estranged son of Dilnavaz, *subjo* leaves for Cavasji's hypertension and nails and lizard for Roshan's illness. Dilnavaz is also in the reflex habit of saying 'touchwood' and touching any wooden item nearby—a table or a chair, whenever she hears about some accident or is just motivated by a desire to avoid anything untoward happening to her family.

In his first book, *The Treatise on General Sociology*, Vilfred Pareto (1848-1923) has raised the issue in much the same vein as Mistry that actions resting on exact knowledge—purely logical or means-ends estimations and judgements are very rare in human affairs. Only a very limited section of actions in society, approximates to logic. The rest is relegated to specific kinds of human propensities, instincts and interests through which mankind seeks material gratification. These are the actions like prayers which are attached to sentiments or subjective desire, often without a definite orientation to ends, which are, in any case, vague, diffused and unattainable. In short, we aspire for such things that have no logic of causality. All this does some good at least psychologically; they have their utility but not their truth. Pareto calls these actions, emanating as they do from primordial human nature, residues.

Pareto examines multitudes of human actions that constitute the outward expressions of sentiments and classifies these residues into six major classes. Class One is the manifestation of sentiments in individuals and in society that tend toward inventiveness and the desire for adventure. Class Two residues encompass the more conservative side of human nature, including loyalty to society's enduring institutions such as family, church, community, and nation. In a society, both have their respective roles and functions and complement each other but what concerns us here is the fact that both these concepts are built around sentiments and not reason.

Another Italian thinker Machiavelli divided humans into two classes—foxes and lions. The qualities he ascribes to these two classes of men resemble quite closely Pareto's Class I and Class II residue types. Men with strong Class I residues are the "foxes," tending to be manipulative, innovative, calculating, and imaginative. Class II men are "lions" who place much more value on traits such as good character and devotion to duty than on sheer wits. They are the defenders of tradition, the guardians of religious dogma, and the protectors of national honour. Indeed, Major Bilimoria, who symbolizes 'Nagarwala' of the real political scandal, appears to be a fox to start with but Gustad remains a lion throughout: both are sentimental fools, however. After the former withdraws himself from the Khodadad Building surreptitiously, Gustad learns a bitter lesson—never to trust friends. And yet Gustad is noble enough to prove himself a true friend not only to Bilimoria and Dinshawji but also to the half-wit Tehmul.

At times, Gustad appears like Roderigo of Shakespeare's *Othello*, who was advised by Iago: "Put money enough in your purse." This is the same line that occurs repeatedly towards the end of Act I and Gustad is asked by Bilimoria to mark it so that the former may be marked by his man, Gulam Mohammad. Roderigo is a poor gentleman—for he is a gentleman, though a "gulled gentleman—he has a sad life in the play, bled white by Iago, disappointed of his hopes . . . a pathetic figure . . . trying to swim in a sea much too rough for him" (Ridley lxvi). Doesn't Bilimoria make Gustad a Roderigo? Tested on the touchstone of rationalism, Gustad's agreeing to see a languishing Bilimoria in Delhi does not appear any whit logical. However, as things unfold themselves later, Bilimoria himself is taken in by bigger foxes.

The Parsi community has been in India for quite a few centuries now and still their total population stands at a few thousands only. Seen from this angle, they can be categorised as an ethnic minority, but the sense of their great heritage, their rich contribution to the country of their adoption, i.e., India, their forward-looking attitude—all these have denied to them a minority syndrome that is normally characterized by low achievements, high crime rate and worry about amalgamation through inter-race marriages etc. (King & Koller 244). Parsis are also alleged to have gained a lot through collusion with the Britishers before independence in India. This is not to discount the valuable contribution made to the independence struggle by stalwarts like

Dadabhai Naoroji and Sir Pherozeshah Mehta. Yet it is a fact that the bulk of the Parsees kept aloof from common Indians on account of their better economic and educational status. In the post-independence India, their partially westernized life-style has ensured the continuation of the wedge between the two communities.

Allowance must be made here for the very ordinary Parsee characters of modest financial standing portrayed by Mistry in the present novel. They retain residues of ordinary prejudices of their group. Durkheim believed: "the fundamental categories of thought have a social origin, and that they owe their necessity and their a priori character to the fact that they are the basis of all intercourse between individuals." (Ginsberg 119). The members of the Parsee community have their thoughts fashioned by inadequate knowledge of the majority community. Dilnavaz is enchanted by the milkman's *choti* but does not know its name. She has a faint idea that some caste sports it. Born of this ignorance is the suspicion of the slum-dwellers whose eyes seem to be threatening to throw the Parsees out.

Sociologists are of the view that "every in-group constructs out-group stereotypes" (Bierstedt 291). This, again, is an illogical construct that effaces differences and upstages oddities at the cost of positive qualities of a group. Therefore, all Maharashtrians are lumped together as 'Maratha buggers' (330). Prejudices take the form of derogatory references like "The Maratha brigade ran like cockroaches" (40). The numerous jokes regarding various communities (70-71) though in good faith, do point to underestimating the value of the out-groups. Beef is humorously considered healthier "because it is holier" (23). The Parsees themselves are at the receiving end when they are referred to as 'crow eaters' (39).

Pheroze Gandhi, who married Indira Gandhi, was a Parsee, so Mistry, despite his commendable objectivity as a writer, bolsters his image. While referring to Nehru's changed mood after the Chinese aggression of 1962, Mistry, going by his penchant for mixing the private with the public, comments, "From now on, he would brook no criticism, take no advice. With his appetite for philosophy and dream lost for ever, he resigned himself to political intrigues and internal squabbles, although signs of his tyrannical ill temper and petulance had emerged even before the China war. His feud with his son-in-law, the thorn in his political side, was well known. Nehru never forgave Feroze Gandhi for exposing scandals in the government; he no longer had any use for defenders of the downtrodden and champions of the poor, roles he had himself once played with great gusto and tremendous success." (11)

Clearly, Mistry also takes on the role of a historian. The novelist is rightly believed to have an edge over the historian in that the latter can give expression to the hidden aspects of social life which evade the historian's pen, as for example, the hopes and aspirations or the fears and tensions of ordinary people. Human impulses such as these manifest themselves only under certain favourable conditions and are taken note of by the historian if at all these affect the power structure and the historian is allowed by the ruler of the land to write about it all. A novelist can, therefore, take cognizance of rumours also as Mistry does in regard to the death of Prime Minister Lal Bahadur Shastri, hours after signing, allegedly under Russian pressure, a settlement with a vanquished Pakistan: "The night the Tashkent Declaration was signed, Shastri died on Soviet soil, less than eighteen months after he became Prime Minister. Some said he had been killed by the Pakistanis, and others suspected a Russian plot. Some even claimed it was the new Prime Minister's supporters who poisoned Shastri, so that her father's dynastic-democratic dream could finally come true." (114)

A novelist also has the means to lend an air of authenticity to what may only be a conjecture to a historian. Now, this interference in the domain of the historian cannot be justified on the basis of rationality because a historian has his well-defined scientific tools to reach a fact while on the other hand, a novelist has no such constraints imposed upon him. The political event that constitutes the plot of this novel pertains to the well-known

Nagarwala scandal that created a lot of dust during the Bangladesh war. While quite a few people believed that Indira Gandhi used the Research and Analysis Wing (RAW), the top-most intelligence agency of the country, to execute her personal agenda, Mistry has put this very information in the mouth of the fictitious RAW operative Major Bilimoria who is shown confined to a hospital bed in a military hospital in Delhi and is able to speak laboriously due to the impact of medicines: "Big surprise . . . she was using RAW like her own private agency. Spying on opposition parties, ministers . . . anyone. For blackmail. Made me sick. Even spying on her own cabinet. One of them prefers little boys. Another takes pictures of himself doing it with women. Bribes, thievery . . . so much going on, Gustad. RAW kept dossiers. On her friends and enemies. Where they went, who they met, what they said, what they ate, what they drank." (270)

A common subject of societal conversation in India is politics. Now, the popular understanding of politics is simplistic rather than rationalistic. A fine specimen of this, couched in figurative language is provided by Gustad-Dinshawji's tête-à-tête: "Where is *madar chod* America now? Not saying one word. Otherwise, if Russia even belches, America protests at the UN. Let Kosygin fart, and America moves a motion in the Security Council" (76). It is not that persons like Gustad are not aware of what goes under the title 'news.' Cautioning his son, he waxes eloquent, "Whatever you read in the paper, first divide by two—for the salt and pepper. From what's left, take off ten percent. Ginger and garlic. And sometimes, depending on the journalist, another five percent for chilli powder. Then, and only then, will you get to the truth free of masala and propaganda" (68). Later, Gustad himself is at the receiving end of the RAW personnel's macabre modus operandi. It is Ghulam Mohammad's turn to remind Gustad of the doubtful nature of news, "You know everything that appears in newspapers is not the truth" (202). In the kind of society to which Gustad belongs, Peerbhoy Paanwala analyses news in his inimitable style for the benefit of his customer-audience.

In such a society, myths are born easily. Thus, Medhiwala Bonesetter, the one who set right Gustad's aching hip, is famed to have 'piercing eyes' because of which the X-ray laboratories suffer in getting business (130). Peerbhoy Paanwala too, is no less than a saintly figure with "his unblinking all-seeing third eye. Sitting cross-legged on his wooden box, he seemed more swami or guru than paanwala, his high forehead furrowed with creases bespeaking ancient wisdom, his large authoritative nose flaring brahminically as he dispensed slices of sagacity in direct discourse or wrapped between betel leaves." This wisdom in betel leaves takes umpteen shapes to "ward off sleep, to promote rest, to create appetites, to rein in an excess of lust, to help digestion, to assist bowel movements, to purify the kidneys, to nullify flatulence, to cure bad breath, to create seductive breath, to fight failing eyesight, to make well the deaf ear, to encourage lucidity of thought, to improve speech, to alleviate the stiffness of joints, to induce longevity, to reduce life expectancy, to mitigate the labour of birthing, to ease the pain of dying—in short, he had a paan for all seasons."

The enthusiasm for deification is quite common. Mr. Rabadi, the 'dogwala idiot,' would like Dustoorji Baria's picture to be drawn on the municipal wall, for he can prescribe remedies for all the ills of life related to health, job, business, social status and even pet animals (288). It is a world in which "roadside latrines become temples and shrines, and temples and shrines become dust and ruin." (338) In this world, where Tatas and Birlas are favoured as against the poor people, Cavasji finds God highly irrational. At a time when the sky is overcast, he admonishes the Almighty: "Monsoon is coming, so you be careful! Year after year, your floods are washing away poor people's huts! Enough now! Where is your fairness? Have you got any brains or not? Flood the Tatas this year! Flood the Birlas, flood the Mafatlals!" (127)

However, when a catastrophe like the Chinese aggression of India takes place, a rare emotional camaraderie is seen. The aggressor is transmuted to the category of a bugbear. "The wicked

Chino will carry you off if you don't finish your food," Dilnavaz would tell her son Darius (9). Even a much lesser problem like the demolition of the boundary wall of Khodadad Building brings about a feeling of camaraderie among people living within and without, regardless of their religious or regional affiliation. In such vital matters of life and death, the survival instinct is at work. One is reminded of the famous simile of freezing porcupines given by Schopenhauer, which "crowd together to save themselves from being frozen to death, but separate again as soon as they feel one another's quills until at length they discover a mean distance at which they can tolerably exist." (Ginsberg 103).

Even though scientists and philosophers have failed to find final answers to the myriad questions of philosophy, a kind of obsession with rationalism, that Eldorado of epistemology has marked the thinking of man much against human experience in certain weak moments. The great apostle of rationalism Descartes took it upon himself to find a body of self-evident truths which could appeal to common sense and the faculty of reasoning. He desired to see the kind of accuracy in philosophy as characterized Mathematics, "prayed for divine illumination, vowing a pilgrimage to the shrine of Loretto in case his prayer should be answered." (Thilly 273).

There are perhaps limits to practical transformation of all human ideas. G.B. Shaw's 'The Revolutionary's Handbook,' a part of his magnum opus *Man and Superman* begins with the promise to unravel the 'golden rule' but deconstructs stating simply, "The golden rule is that there is no golden rule." Major Bilimoria has learnt while working in RAW that one must not trust anyone howsoever near and dear. Unfortunately, if the worldly-wise Major had stuck to this golden principle, it would have been a rational approach and he would have saved his skin, but acting on impulse and taken in by the majestic charm of the Prime Minister, he signed his confession. (277) While the Major meets his doom at the end of the novel, Sohrab's estrangement and Roshan's illness also end. However, this latter happy development coincides with the last magic rites conducted by Miss Kutpitia before the laboratory of magic goes up in flames. The writer seems to be trying to achieve some kind of suspension of disbelief with regard to the miraculous impact of the magic.

All this brings us to the moot question: Why does man leave the straight path of reason and get fascinated by the labyrinthine maze of sentimentality instead? The answer, if it can be called an answer, is provided by the footpath artist, "You see, I don't like to weaken anyone's faith. Miracle, magic, mechanical trick, coincidence—does it matter what it is, as long as it helps? Why analyse the strength of the imagination, the power of suggestion, power of auto-suggestion, the potency of psychological pressures?" (289)

Chapter 5

A Fine Balance: Lest the Apple Cart be Upset!

Rohinton Mistry's second novel *A Fine Balance* stands out in comparison with *Such a Long Journey* on several counts such as a wider scope that includes large chunks of non-Parsi population. For the first time, Mistry deals with the lives of rural folk and portrays graphically the endemic problem of caste-based hatred so very characteristic of the Indian rural scene. Besides, it probes in depth the lifestyle of the subaltern and the bourgeois classes at a historical moment when the country was subjected to the traumatic experience of an emergency regime for the first time in India.

The title 'A Fine Balance' is quite cryptic in that it says and unsays at the same time and could be deconstructed to deliver several interpretations: The writer may be pointing out the right kind of balance in this world that is available to his characters or the one they could be searching for in their lives. The word 'fine' is amenable to several meanings. So, does the writer mean the balance presented here is fine in the sense of being delicate that could be upset easily? Or is the balance fine in the sense of beautiful? The word 'fine' also refers to that which is 'difficult to see or describe' (Oxford), so the writer's intention could be satirical also.

There are references to "hope enough to balance our despair or we would be lost," as Vasantrao Valmik tells Dina Dalal towards the end of the novel (553), but the kind of balance one witnesses in the lives of the people like Dina, Om, Ishvar, Maneck, Ashraf chacha, the monkey man, the rent collector, the beggarmaster et al cannot be called fine in the sense of beautiful. It may be a very thin, almost insignificant kind of thread that joins together their physical, emotional and spiritual selves. Not much value is attached to the lives of these people in this populous nation where the demons of political corruption, moral hypocrisy and social injustice shatter the dreams of ordinary people.

The author's intention would be expressed better if the title were to end with an exclamation mark, i.e., A Fine Balance! That would bring out the writer's sarcasm writ large over the fictional canvas. Or the title could have a question mark—A Fine Balance? That would express the writer's bewilderment in locating a semblance of balance in the given circumstances. Such a change in the title alone would indicate the sentiment of the author who comments obliquely on the *chalta hai* mindset of the suffering people pulling on somehow with their insignificant lives finding solace at times in philosophical musings.

The story of this voluminous novel begins with the entry into an unnamed city (ostensibly Mumbai) of Ishvar and his nephew Om, who are both *Chamar* by caste but tailors by training. They have come from a remote village, bringing memories of torture and brutality at the hands of the upper caste landowners. On the local train, they happen to meet a young college student Maneck Kohlah who has come from the hills to study in Mumbai. The destination of all of them is the middle-aged widow Dina Dalal's house where the tailors stitch clothes on contract basis and Maneck stays as a paying guest. She has decided to stay single and not be dependent on her condescending elder brother Nusswan. Meanwhile, the emergency is imposed and what follows is a string of unsavoury experiences for all. One day, Om and Ishvar find the *jhoparpatti*, they stay in, razed to the ground for the sake of beautification of the city. They try every conceivable shelter but have to rest content with the narrow entrance to a chemist's shop. One night, they are picked up along with other shelterless labourers and beggars and forcibly taken away to be confined to a construction site. Their pleas that they are trained tailors fall on deaf ears.

They are able to purchase freedom, courtesy a certain beggarmaster whom they meet after cultivating friendship with a beggar Shankar, a fellow-prisoner at the camp. Back at Dina's, they are allowed to stay put in the verandah. An understanding develops among the residents of the flat now. Ishvar persuades Om to get married and both of them proceed to their native village for the purpose where they are once again taken away forcibly to a family planning camp and vasectomy operations are performed on them. Their old adversary Thakur Dharamsi happens to be the influential politician supervising the camp. One complaining glance from Om and the latter is castrated as well. Ishvar also develops post-operation problems and severe infection costs him his legs. In Mumbai, Maneck has left for home but he is not able to come back because of his failure to get admission to the college for the next course. The landlord has Dina evicted for flouting the tenancy norms by running a tailoring business. She has to go back to her brother much against her wishes.

Om and Ishvar return but neither of them is fit for work, so they take to begging. They are still in touch with Dina who helps them off and on and away from the sight of Nusswan and his family. An even more tragic fate awaits Maneck. He gets a job in Dubai and visits India only in 1984 to perform the last rites of his father. He happens to know of the murder in police custody of his college friend Avinash from an old newspaper which he chances to read at home. The report is given as a run-up to the suicide of Avinash's three sisters because of the inability of their old father to arrange dowry for their marriage. A few dialogues with his mother and he is sure he won't be able to stay there to run the family business. On his way back to Dubai, he makes a halt at Mumbai, where the tragic fate of Om and Ishvar comes as the final blow to his sensitive soul and he commits suicide.

A Fine Balance is basically a realistic tragedy in which the humble dreams and aspirations of the common people lie shattered like a house of cards. Destiny or whosoever dispenses justice in this fictional world has the least qualms about justice and fair play. Characters good at heart meet an undeserved doom. True to his own nature, Mistry has imbued almost all the characters in the novel with noble sentiments. They are sensitive and reasonably intelligent people. Even though some of them have an humble background, they do possess certain moral standard. Thus, Dina Dalal tries to be strict towards her workers as per the instructions of Mrs. Gupta, but her mind is torn in conflict when she tries to set the dividing "line between compassion and foolishness, kindness and weakness" because that would be her selfish standpoint. From their point of view, it might be a line between "mercy and cruelty, consideration and callousness" (376). This very Dina sees pattern on the quilt as symbolic of life. The unfinished corner of the quilt remains symbolic of the lack of balance. This quilt made so lovingly provides a delicate balance to the legless body of Ishvar, the tailor-turned-beggar. Her end is from where she began, under the watchful eyes of her elder brother, her position no better than a domestic help to Mrs. Ruby Nusswan.

Except for Nusswan and his wife, the middle-class characters in *A Fine Balance* are not snobs. A liberal outlook that treats all people equally in society marks them. In this, they remind the reader of Gustad Noble of *Such a Long Journey*, who treats the half-wit Tehmul as his son only. Even when the latter is found in an awkward situation at a brothel, Gustad comes to his rescue without any consideration of his own status. In a way, such characters are representative of the writer's compassionate nature. Not only the ruralites Om and Ishvar but even Maneck Kohlah coming from a middle class Parsi family has no scruples dealing with the beggar Shankar. He, along with Dina Dalal, joins Shankar's funeral procession. But the harshly realistic world of Rohinton Mistry has no scope for poetic justice. Therefore, such people also lose out in the game of life.

Ishvar Darji is a very honest, respectful and kind-hearted person who behaves in a very cultured manner. His nephew Om may, at times, act moody and think in terms of wresting business from his employer Dina Dalal but his uncle takes these traits as signs of immaturity and chastises him. Whereas Ishvar has reconciled himself to his destiny, Om craves sometimes for revenge on Thakur Dharmsi who is responsible for the undoing of his family. In the scheme of things, however, both uncle and nephew remain at the receiving end for no fault of theirs.

Pauperization, both financial and emotional, is a hard fact of life for the leading characters of *A Fine Balance*, be it Dina Dalal in Mumbai, the Kohlahs in the hills or the low-caste family of Dukhi back in the village. A very clear manifestation of the trend is to be found in the case of the rent collector who is shown standing with a tin-pot to collect coins at the gate of the very building which he once used to lord over, on behalf of the landlord. Om and Ishvar are also reduced to beggary. The once proud Dina Dalal has to be at the mercy of her brother again. Other characters like the monkey man were always at the fringe. Life has certainly been cruel to these people.

Apart from these characters, *A Fine Balance* portrays some grotesque figures also in the vein of Charles Dickens's memorable characters Uriah Heep and Fagin who can be compared to Rajaram and the 'Beggarmaster' respectively. Readers come across Rajaram, the hair-collector with his trade-mark 'Namaskar,' who changes vocations from a hair-collector to a forecaster and even commits murder, unwittingly as per his own version, to stay afloat in this world. He is the one who has the knack to swim with the tide and treat every problem as 'a small obstacle.' In the last scene, he dons the mantle of a Bal Baba with that lover of letters Vasantrao Valmik, the advocate turned speech writer, as his assistant. But Rajaram's is the art of chicanery. Through such a character, Mistry has a fling at the society in which the innocent are punished but the cheats have a field day.

The Beggarmaster, with his briefcase of coins chained to his hand, is another bizarre character. His trade is rooted in ruthlessness and a clear evidence is found when he takes away the monkey man's children, maims and blinds them and turns them into beggars for which he deservedly pays with his life in the end. But Mistry's compassion knows no bounds and even here he shows pangs of conscience troubling the beggarmaster when the latter discovers Shankar to be his step-brother. This very beggarmaster finds a completeness, a calmness, in fact, a perfect balance between life and death in a burning pyre. That is why he even goes to strangers' cremations (495).

Mistry delineates ugly aspects of life in such gory detail that one starts suspecting if he relishes what seems nauseating to an ordinary observer, but all this is done to emphasize reality which acts as a drag on any kind of balance in life. Let us take up the scene where the village Pandit clarifies Dukhi's doubts following the latter's son having sought education through trespass in the village school. The way the Pandit conducts some of the bodily business is an example:

> Pandit Lalluram raised his eyebrows and rubbed his big toe. Nodding, he kneaded sweat and dirt into black bit that rolled off his fingers. . . . Still silent, Pandit Lalluram sniffed the fingers which had finished massaging his big toe. He pivoted on one buttock and broke wind. Dukhi leaned back to allow it free passage, wondering what penalty might adhere to the offence of interfering with the waft of brahminical flatus. . . . He leaned sideways and blew a thick stream of mucus out of his nose on to the dry earth. The impact of its landing raised a tiny puff of dust. He rubbed his nose and sighed again. (112)

Mistry's penchant for realism drives him to paint the most natural actions which are normally neglected by the writers. The sight of destitute people lining the railway track in the morning in an attempt to attend to nature's call is a common sight in India. In such a scene presented in the novel, Om, Ishvar and Rajaram are shown cutting scatological jokes. The reference is to a certain sect of black magic practitioners who eat human excreta to attain magical powers, while Om thinks aloud of starting a shit-collection business as it is so freely available there: "Ready made lunches, teatime snacks, hot and steaming." (206-7)

A sordid reality portrayed in the novel is in the form of commerce in invalid humans—both grown ups and children. The site is the labour camp set up during emergency on the pattern of the concentration camps in Soviet Russia as described by Solzhenitsyn in *The Gulag Archipelago*. Here, in the Indian camp are the pavement dwellers who are brought in forcibly. The camp-incharge has devised a plan with the help of a certain Facilitator to make easy money. Those found unfit for work are to be handed over to the Beggarmaster, for a price, of course. The process reminds one of business in vegetable market on any working day:

> Monkey-man was still comatose from his head injury, and Beggarmaster refused to take him. But he wanted the children; they had real potential, he said. The little boy and girl resisted removal, weeping and clinging to their motionless uncle. They had to be dragged away when the truck was ready to leave.
>
> The Facilitator and foreman balanced the debits and credits with a rebate towards the next delivery. Then there was a short delay. The foreman insisted that clothing issued on arrival be removed before departure—he had to account for every article to his superiors. (361)

The funeral procession of the beggar Shankar presents another abominable scene. The novelist describes "the assembly of crippled, blinded, armless, legless, diseased and faceless individuals on the pavement" (493). The funeral procession proceeds at a snail's pace because "the deformities of some had atrophied their bodies, reducing them to a froglike squat; they swung along using their arms as levers. A few could only manage the sideways shuffle of a crab. Others, doubled over, crawled forward on their hands and feet, their behinds raised in the air like camels' humps" (494).

Apart from these ugly aspects, the common problems faced by people in the metropolis have been given wide coverage. The hardships encountered by Om and Ishvar in securing a shelter befit a saga. Sometimes it is the awning of Nawaz's house, at another the entrance to a chemist store. Ishvar is experienced enough to tell Dina, "Next time I go searching for accommodation, you should come with me, see how families live. Eight, nine, or ten people in a small room. Sleeping one over the other on big shelves, from floor to ceiling, like third-class railway berths. Or in cupboard, or in the bathroom. Surviving like goods in a warehouse." (461) How can these conditions help one to maintain a sound balance of mind or body?

The village from which Om and Ishvar come, is no idyllic paradise either. Inhuman oppression of the *Chamar* family starts when Dukhi decides to train his sons Ishvar and Narayan as tailors. Narayan's assertion to vote freely offends Thakur Dharamsi no end and for this grave offence, Narayan is hanged. Other untouchables are thrashed, their women raped and huts burnt down. Madness does not stop here. Finally, Dukhi, his wife and Narayan's wife and daughters are burnt alive. The purpose behind allowing such a large canvas to the depiction of poverty, deprivation, dirt and squalor that pervades the Indian scene seems to be to underline the enormity of the problem. Where is the hope for a balance, a fine one at that?

The novelist castigates the political leadership of the country for all the ills that befell the nation during the run of the ill-conceived emergency. As in *Such a Long Journey*, Mistry takes to task the politicians and their minions because he holds politicians at the highest level responsible for being obsessed with their selfish interests only at the cost of millions of people in society. The gory incidents of the Emergency days were possible only with the help of people like Thakur Dharamsi. Mistry satirises the way people are forcibly brought in for the Prime Minister's rally. They are promised food and a meagre allowance but even that commitment is not fully honoured.

On another occasion, Om and Ishvar are forcibly taken away as ticketless travellers even when they have valid tickets and are just taking a short-cut out of the railway platform. Rajaram, the hair-collector slaps his forehead on coming to know of their ordeal and remarks, "Some people travel all their lives without buying single ticket. And you two get caught on the first day. Even with tickets." To this, the two reply, "Must be a new policy because of Emergency." They are let off after they have performed fifty 'uthak-baithaks,' because there is no space left in jails which are full with political opponents of the Prime Minister (181-82).

Overmuch detail of reality does not go down well with the readers. In order to lighten the atmosphere, the writer resorts to a satiric undercurrent that is the hallmark of the novel. At another level, what is laughable also suggests its incongruity and incompleteness, sufficient to turn it into an eyesore—again something off-balance. The life sketch of the abominable rent-collector Ibrahim is compressed in the following sentences:

> Ibrahim, the son of ageing parents, became a husband, then a father. And the role of rent-collector began to sprout branches too. He was appointed the landlord's spy, blackmailer, deliverer of threats, and all-round harasser of tenants. His job now included the uncovering of hidden dirt in his six buildings, secrets like extramarital affairs, and he was taught by his employer how to convert adultery into rent increases—the guilty parties would never protest or dare to mention the Rent Act. When the situation demanded, Ibrahim could play the pleader and cajoler, if the landlord went too far and there was legalistic retaliation. The rent-collector's tears would convince the tenant to back down, to have mercy on the poor beleaguered landlord, a martyr to modern-day housing, who had never meant any harm in the first place.
>
> To sort out the multiple roles in Ibrahim's repertoire, the folder's pouches and compartments were indispensable. At this stage in his career, however, he began to feel the increasing hindrance of his sweet automatic smile. Delivering threats and dire warning while smiling pleasantly, he discovered, was not a good strategy. If he could have modified it to a menacing smile, that would have been perfect. But the muscles in question were beyond his control. (86)

There is a take on the superstitious people also. Ibrahim, the rent-collector develops the habit of getting 'divine advice' for his worldly affairs from a certain communicating-cow, bedecked and trained for the purpose, by a roadside fortune-teller. Unfortunately, this cow goes berserk one day. "For a moment, the spectators thought the cow was just responding a bit more energetically than usual to the question. Then she tossed him to the ground, trampling him thoroughly. Now they realized it was not a part of the prophecy procedure" (88).

Similarly, the substitution of the band party on the occasion of the Narayan's marriage back in the village creates a ridiculous situation. Under pressure from Thakur Dharamsi, the village musicians back out and a new party is called in but they do not know the traditional tunes played on such occasions. The elders resent the 'alien tunes' but what is worse, the womenfolk consider the new tunes inauspicious for the birth of children. (138)

Mistry's observant eye does not leave out even minor prejudices of people. Thus, the Parsees' colour-prejudice is brought to the fore when Mrs. Sodawalla is reported to be impressed by the young Farokh's light pigmentation. "Not white like a European ghost, she told her friends, but fair and golden." Some balance indeed! So, the Sodawalla family takes a 'tactical vacation' to visit the hill station so that Miss Aban could meet Farokh Kohlah. "The strategy produced the desired results. Aban fell in love with Farokh Kohlah and the natural beauty of the place." (202)

The novel satirises the shallow morality of the middle class. Dina Dalal, after having lost her husband, develops relations with Fredoon, who is more interested in physical contact. But the marital sanctity of the bed is uppermost in Dina's mind. She would not hear of going to bed with him even though her husband had been dead for six months. A *fine balance* is sought to be struck when she agrees to satisfy his desire in standing position only. Mistry takes the practical joke-type affair a little too far when he shows Fredoon devising contraption with hanging pillows etc. to make the experience less taxing and more enjoyable. But the experiment is not a success so that the much sought-after fine balance remains elusive in this imperfect world.

Mistry seems to laugh at the fate of his own creations, who lead life as worms and insects. No doubt, they settle down somehow in life and continue to exist, except for Maneck who fails to strike a compromise with life and throws himself in front of a speeding railway engine but the reconciliation with life is borne out of compulsion only. Outwardly, they may seem to be taking things in their stride as Om and Ishvar are seen cracking jokes even in beggars' garb towards the close of the novel, but one cannot write off lightly the dreams that Om had about Shanti or the ones which his uncle had about their future.

One might feel satisfied about the fine balance in the relations between the ruralites Om and Ishvar on the one hand and the urbanites Dina and Maneck on the other. The bonhomie reaches the climax when Dina, in a bid to avoid suspicion of the landlord's snooping agent Ibrahim, falsely announces that Ishvar is her husband. However, it must be remembered here that this comment was made out of compulsion and their relationship remained strictly that of employees and employer.

Towards the close of the novel, it seems the author finds his writing skills no match to the unimaginable grief and misery in this world. At this juncture, Mistry sheds the canonical restraint of satire and makes his characters forgo the fine balance of mind. Maneck is aghast with the terrible mental tension that the revelation of events surrounding Avinash's disappearance brings. It is followed by macabre suicide of his three sisters and Maneck wails:

> What sense did the world make? Where was God, the Bloody Fool? Did He have no notion of fair and unfair? Couldn't He read a simple balance sheet? He would have been sacked long ago if He were managing a corporation, the things He allowed to happen. (585)

Add to this, Maneck's disenchantment with his own family, the pauperisation of Om, Ishvar and Dina, the members of his adopted family. All these are too much to bear for him. In a fit of extreme despair, he commits suicide.

This may have appeared "morbid," "startling and unconventional" to some critics (Kapadia 133), but it clearly reflects the thinking of the author that the kind of balance between hope and despair maintained by Om and Ishvar is not possible for all. To

Maneck, the fine balance comes in life only in perfect stillness, as is seen in the case of glowing coals used to cook *kababs* in the Vishram Restaurant. "Starting small, with modest heat, then growing to powerful red incandescence, spitting and snapping, their tongue soft flame crackling, all heat and passion, transforming, threatening, devouring. And then—the subsidence. Into mellow warmth, compliance, and finally, a perfect stillness" (600).

Another critic underlines the moral of maintaining a fine balance, which, for Dina is the balance of patriarchy, for Ishvar and Om the balance between their low-caste origin and their newly found *darji* status and the balance in the life of nations which India lost during emergency. As for the other paradigms of balance pointed out earlier, she has this to say: "It is this fine balance which if the persons concerned learn to master, helps them to lead a relatively peaceful, happy life; if they fail, it tips them over into the abyss" (Bharucha 166). We must pause here and consider this "relatively peaceful happy life." From the account given in the novel, one gathers it is that of a dependent for Dina, of mendicants for Ishvar and Om, a pseudo-sanyasi for Rajaram. The alternative 'abyss' is death and deliverance from the circle of life for Maneck. Surely, none of these is the cherished ideal of the novelist.

A Fine Balance is a powerful satire on the post-independence political and social dispensation in India, whose decisions affect man in the street. The first experiment with the constitutional provision of emergency undertaken by self-serving politicians in the country was a disaster and the novel details the events quite graphically. To look for a balance in that historical aberration would tantamount to the proverbial search for a needle in the haystack. Even otherwise also there are myriad restraints to a just and equitable existence in this country with its age-old caste prejudices to which the modern lust for lucre has added another dimension. Mistry has successfully portrayed the reality without mincing words and in doing so he has lodged a powerful protest against the status quo. In an interview with Narmeen Sheikh, he refers to the choice between novel and protest song which makes clear his penchant for protest. *A Fine Balance* fits admirably into Ian Jack's definition of satire: "Satire is born of the instinct to protest; it is protest become art" (Cuddon 780) *A Fine Balance* is certainly an artistic and caustic comment on a futile search for stability and meaning in life in the given context.

Chapter 6

Family Matters: Practising Values in Troubled Times

Rohinton Mistry's third novel *Family Matters* has been rightly acclaimed as a masterpiece. The writer's humanity and compassion, which also found expression in his earlier two novels *Such a Long Journey* and *A Fine Balance* and in different stories of the collection entitled *Tales from Firozsha Baag,* finds beautiful expression in this novel. Despite a simpler diction as compared to that used in *A Fine Balance*, the present work has a subtle depth which speaks of Mistry's master craftsmanship. Behind the normal ebb and flow of life depicted in this novel lies the sorry state of society in which human values come under strain due to financial predicament.

Yezad is the chief protagonist even though other characters also receive considerable attention of the author. Major upheavals occur in his life due to the mental struggle following disregard of the value-code that he held dear in his life. Starting with his resolve to maintain distance from his father-in-law, he is pitted against circumstances that make demands on his conscience. Willy-nilly, he becomes an accomplice in the chain of events leading to the death of his employer Mr. Kapoor. After this, his life becomes a story of repentance.

Before we proceed any further, it would be pertinent at this point to go over the storyline. The plot of the novel revolves around a lower middle class Parsi family of Bombay (now Mumbai). The head of the family Nariman Vakeel is a retired professor of English literature. In his late seventies, he suffers from Parkinson's disease about which his step-daughter Coomy is more concerned than his step-son Jal. He lives with them in a building named Chateau Felicity. Both siblings, though well past their marriageable age, are still single. They are the children of Palonji Contractor, the former deceased husband of his wife Yasmeen, who is also no more. Nariman and Yasmeen's daughter Roxana is married to Yazed and is blessed with two young sons—Murad and Jehangir. This family lives in Pleasant Villa which was presented to them by the professor.

The story opens with the concern shown about the professor's health by Jal and Coomy. The concern is not misplaced because soon the old man falls while crossing the road and breaks his ankle. The occasion leads to a slanging match between Nariman and step-children regarding the professor's beloved Lucy who made public demonstration of her love for him. Years ago, both Lucy and Yasmeen died together in a freak accident. The professor is taken to the hospital and put in cast. After a two-day stay there, he is brought back home in an ambulance. Later, the doctor attending on him says the ankle would take some more weeks to get right. The news dampens Coomy's spirits as she is already fed up with looking after the old man, particularly at moments of nature's call. So, a week after the fall, the professor is shifted to his daughter Roxana's small flat and assured that it was for a few days only. Surprisingly, she had not been informed about the accident earlier. As the days drag on, Coomy's fertile brain hatches an ingenious plan, according to which Jal deliberately hammers the roof of Nariman's room so that the plaster falls down.

Thereafter, both of them visit Roxana and deliver the disturbing news of a leaking overhead tank the water from which has seeped through the roof making it impossible to host Nariman there in near future. As expected, Yezad and Roxana are a worried lot now. They want some financial support from Coomy which the latter refuses straightaway leading to exchange of some unsavoury words between the two parties. To save her face however, Coomy engages an amateur handyman Edul residing in the same building to repair the 'leaking roof.' The novice that he is, an iron beam while being hoisted up, falls down on Edul and Coomy, killing the two there and then.

Meanwhile, Yezad, under financial burden due to the upkeep of his father-in-law, tries gambling, courtesy Villie Cardmaster, the Matka-queen residing nearby. He does win initially but soon the police enforce a ban on all Matka operations in the city. Yezad's son Murad saves bus fare by walking on foot rather than commuting by bus to the school. Jehangir, in his innocence, starts accepting bribe from his rich class-mates, whose home work he is entrusted to monitor on behalf of his teacher. This misdemeanour is found out soon and his father called to the school for discussion. Finally, Yezad resorts to a devious plan to raise funds. In a politically vitiated climate, he reports to his boss the fictitious demand from Shiv Sena activists for money in lieu of permission to keep 'Bombay' instead of 'Mumbai' in the name of the firm. Mr. Kapoor is in deep love with every old thing about Bombay. He won't hear of such a thing and instead would part with money. On the appointed day, however, real Shiv Sena men descend demanding change of name but before they have spoken out, Mr. Kapoor castigates them for their earlier demand and throws the money at them at which they take offence and murder Mr. Kapoor. Yezad is rightly shaken by this sudden turn of events and considers himself responsible for Kapoor's murder. The all-round downslide makes Yezad turn to prayers to find some solace.

Coomy's death brings about the badly needed turnaround in the lives of these people. Jal prepares a plan that is finally put into operation. According to it, Yezad's flat is sold for forty lakh rupees. Some of the amount is spent on the renovation of the seven-room house in Chateau Felicity and the rest is kept in bank deposits, the interest from which is sufficient to see all of them through life. All of them now shift to this spacious accommodation. After a year, Nariman passes away due to Parkinson's disease confounded by a rather imperfect handling by the professional nurses. The Epilogue, entirely Jehangir's point of view, shows Yezad passing his time in reading religious scriptures and praying. He is now a self-righteous Zoroastrian Parsi who frowns upon any sign of modernity. However, in Jehangir's eyes he is a bigot only.

This simple story with its share of ups and downs has a disturbing undercurrent in which all sorts of values—individual, familial, social and spiritual—are problematized. The issue naturally relates to our comprehension of values. A value is what is considered important in society. Ever since society came into existence, the values too were created. They have become an important part not just of social life but also of life at the individual level. Values are necessary for the moral and spiritual growth of man. These are like bench-marks for personal conduct and social interaction. Values as ideals lead one to the highest goal of self-realization besides helping to evolve a comfortable equation with the society in which an individual lives.

Value, per se, is a multi-disciplinary concept with philosophical, ethical, spiritual, aesthetic, psychological and sociological moorings. Taking a cue from the psychologists, we can say that the values are motivating factors of the 'sociogenic' variety which are adopted or learnt as against the biological ones like hunger, sex etc. that are innate. As a member of a society, every person has different needs which act as a drive or motivating factor. Thus, the trait of human sympathy and help to the needy is explained as a 'nurturance' need. Similarly, the trait of social fellowship comes from the 'affiliation' need. The Marxist school also locates 'the source of axiological attitude in the social character of human activity' (Petrovsky 325).

From the philosophical angle, the questions as to what is right and what is wrong have always vexed thinking minds. Something that appears right to a person may not appear so to another. In such circumstances, the ethical rightness assumes two faces—'subjective right' and 'objective right,' as Bertrand Russell would say. Now, whereas subjective right is clear and definite, the objective right or good is indefinable because it depends upon a faculty of ethical intuition that some admit of whereas others do not. At best, we can say that objective good is that which is considered so by the majority of people in a society. Russell tends to discount moral intuition because it can be deconstructed to mean social criticism or praise plus personal emotions of love and hate.

Apart from this universal classification of value system, there are the values typical of a community at a point of time in history. Over centuries of existence on the Indian mainland, the Parsis have, by and large, adapted themselves to the local milieu. We find minor variations of language, dress etc. when we compare them with other people. However, expecting them to have some specific cultural icons and traits is quite natural. The most distinguishing matrix is provided by their religious practices and Mistry has a keen eye for them.

Going over the history of the Parsi community, we find that the period before the independence of the country was crucial to the development of the community and its outlook. It is common knowledge that the Parsis cooperated with the British and came to be seen as their cohorts. This, in turn, led to a certain highbrow attitude among them which alienated them from the bulk of the Indian populace. After the country gained independence, the Parsis, who were quite well-off economically, withdrew themselves into a cocoon, so to say, and devoted themselves mainly to economic activity. Those who found it difficult to adjust to the new reality crossed the shores of the country to settle abroad or nursed dreams of migrating to western countries. Yezad could not go to Canada but his botched plan did leave a scar on his psyche.

While these conditions have left an imprint on the social psyche of Parsis, the Parsis also try their best to impart knowledge of their religion and value system to the young. These efforts do not necessarily succeed at all times. Yezad used to tell his sons the story of his father's valour in displaying loyalty to the bank in which he worked during fierce riots in the city. For this, he was rewarded with a clock that hung in their house and which Yezad zealously guarded as a valuable symbol of honesty and bravery of his late father. Whereas the mythical story of

Faridoon and Zuhaak as told by Nariman to the grandchildren symbolises the eternal nature of the struggle between good and evil, the heroic deed of Yezad's father is brought in to convince the sons of the modern relevance and desire to live by that ideal. But the self-same Yezad minded when his father-in-law told mythical tales to his sons. Pitted against the traditional mode of value impartation was the modern individualistic complex harboured by Yezad that his son was getting distanced from him in this way. Left to themselves, the children depended upon Enid Blyton's books to adopt their role models and reference points—something over which Yezad frets and frowns again fearing children would develop an unhealthy mindset. Roxana, on the other hand, feels proud of her son feeding his grandfather (108), proof enough that the children basically have tender and loving nature. In dealing with their children, Mrs. and Mr. Chenoy show difference of approach

Different types of values apart, the moot question is how man adopts value system in life. If we delve deep into the nature of value-system, we shall find that even when a value is considered to be objective and ultimate, it finally depends for compliance on individual volition. The will of a person with superficial or shallow faith in the value system is bound to dissipate in the face of trying circumstances. Selfishness decides in an overwhelming majority the level of faith in values. The psychologists describe the immediate action of an agent in terms of 'activation' of the central nervous system. This activation depends upon various factors like external stimuli, internal emotions and cognitive factors and their interaction. On the whole, it can be said that value orientation develops as one assimilates social experiences. It also decides personal goals, ideals, interests and traits.

There are times when different motives compete for the attention of man. Also sometimes, our imperfect understanding of values leads to erosion of faith in them followed by incomplete compliance or the total lack of it. Again, at times, one has to deliberate internally for considerable length of time to sort out a conflict. This means even moral values strive to seek rational ground for their nourishment. It is not something new because such efforts were made by the hedonists and the stoics of the post-Aristotelian times also. In the twentieth century, Bertrand Russell echoes similar sentiments, "it is as easy, if not easier to influence emotions by argument as to influence intellectual convictions" (Russell 88). There could be a firm resolution or frustration at not being able to go by one motive or transform the motive into concrete action due to circumstances beyond one's control. *Family Matters* presents an ideal study of the fluctuating commitment to values in the face of odds of different kinds. Economic constraints play as great a role in diluting dedication to family values as does the muddled understanding of moral and social values.

Among the external factors having a bearing on the operation of the value code is the milieu. Of all the characters in *Family Matters*, Yezad is the one whose professional life has been depicted in detail. As such, he should be prone to the influences of other communities at his workplace and public spots. He is fortunate to have got a humane employer in Mr. Kapoor whom he also respects for his intellectual leanings, something rare for a businessman. In contrast, Mrs. Kapoor is a shrewd lady who would make a *pucca* businessman of our times. Kapoor is irretrievably linked emotionally to Bombay and the name of his shop, viz., Bombay Sports Goods Emporium does not seem to have been selected casually. He cherishes the memory of old Bombay through paintings and pictures preserved over a long period by him and laments the depredation brought about by the changing times. Being aware of similarity of Yezad's interests, Mr. Kapoor presents him some valuable pictures from his personal collection and Yezad is appreciative of the spirit of sacrifice behind this gesture.

Not just pictures, Mr. Kapoor also loves the people of Bombay for their cosmopolitan spirit. A Hindu himself, he has least qualms in celebrating Christmas or other festivals belonging to different communities. This approach is diametrically opposite to Yezad's when, egged on by his orthodox Parsi circle, he arranges for the immersion of non-Zorastrian images in sea waters. Kapoor also tries his hand at being one of the myriad Bombayites, commuting daily by local trains. A novice in this art, he suffers but does not complain. It is a philosophical decision, as he explains to Yezad, "I want to embrace everything my city has to offer. I want to mingle with her people, be part of that crush of bodies in the streets and trains and buses. Become one with the organic whole that is Bombay. That's where my redemption lies" (346). What is a philosophical decision for Kapoor is fantastic rhetoric for Yezad. The motivation for this experiment came from a common platform scene in which the daily passengers helped a latecomer chasing the train to board it. But when Kapoor tries to savour the same spirit, the daily commuters just laugh at him and do not extend the helping hand. The reason, as he analyses it, is the fine clothes and shoes that he puts on. So, he would now get ill-fitting cheap clothes from the pavement vendors (348). Kapoor's experiment with a gift-delivering live Santa Claus in his shop evokes a lukewarm response. His search for the values of fellowship and camaraderie comes to an end when Yezad treacherously hatches a heinous plot to extract money from him taking advantage of the fear psychosis created by the Shiv Sena. But Kapoor never compromises on values dear to him. He has the guts to throw money in the face of the 'extortionists' rather than talk peace with the people who want to change the cosmopolitan character of his dear Bombay city. He becomes a martyr to a cause.

Husain is another colleague working in the same emporium. He lost members of his family in the post-Babri riots that rocked Bombay for a long time. Mr. Kapoor, himself a victim of the 1947 riots that accompanied the vivisection of India, tries not to remind Husain of the riots. Husain hardly retains the bitterness of the past, which could have been a normal phenomenon in any ordinary mortal. Another humane character is Vilas, who works in the adjoining book shop and as a side-job, writes letters for the illiterate migrant labourers who come to Bombay from far-off places to earn a livelihood. Thus, the total influence of the individuals working with Yezad should be positive.

What, however, is more relevant here is the way personal, familial and social values change under the pressure of various factors. The change is a fact of human history as Dr. S. Radhakrishnan, while studying the ancient value systems in the garb of religions, comments, "The breakdown of a society is generally due to a failure to devise adequate responses to new challenges to a failure to retain the voluntary allegiance of the common people who, exposed to new winds of thought and criticism, are destitute of faith, though afraid of scepticism." (Gupta 98) A sceptic, whether of religious or social variety, fears not just the disapproval of others if he were to voice his views but also has problem arising from loss of faith that had acted earlier as a firm support for him. This is exactly Yezad's predicament. All is not well with Yezad's world. Financial crunch deals a body blow to the value system cherished by almost all the characters.

At times, *Family Matters* seems to be all about financial matters. The best-known family value in India is the respect for the elderly. When the *ghatis* bring home the injured Nariman for the first time, Coomy wishes to pay *bakshish* to the labourers at the rate at which they lift sacks of rice or wheat. After all, "what difference did it make in terms of labour, whether they were lifting Pappa or a gunny of rice or furniture?" (50) Moving over to Roxana's world, we find that she keeps in her house different envelopes that hold amounts meant for different expenditures. It is futile to expect her husband to receive the ailing patriarch smilingly. So, we have almost a tug-of-war between Coomy and Roxana over the issue of looking after their indisposed father. Even God is falsely blamed for what has been done to the roof above their heads by Jal and Coomy themselves (184). Not surprisingly, nemesis visits Coomy as the manifestation of poetic justice. However, the adage 'Blood is thicker than water' proves partially true in her case as despite her abominable scheming, Coomy does think of her cousins Murad and Jehangir for whose wedding days, she has kept two pairs of gold cufflinks and two sets of shirt studs. These are discovered after her death. (484)

As in the other novels of Mistry, people belonging to the lower middle class have a formidable existence. Their life is beset with a thousand and one problems: their clocks stop, the taps run dry at six in the morning, their grocers cheat them regularly and getting adequate accommodation is well-nigh impossible. In this crowded city, even *kholis* in a modest *chawl* are rented out in shifts of 8 to 12 hours (138). The train travel for the daily commuters involves no less than Tarzan's antics (137). In these trying circumstances, Yezad's delicate balance of family budget is upset by the compulsion of looking after an injured father-in-law. With no hope from any quarter, he is driven to hatch a heinous plot to extract money from his employer Mr. Kapoor. The ethical values of trust and integrity are given a short shrift.

The obsession with purity competes with the universal value placed on reciprocity in love. For one, the reader clearly sees the change in value perspective in the treatment meted out by Nariman to his lady-love Lucy or later by Nariman's children to him. The plot is mum about Nariman's decision to marry Yasmin even when he loved Lucy. Did he buckle down under parents' pressure? If so, he bade farewell to the chivalrous conventions of love even as he fulfilled the demands of the orthodox Parsi society in going by the wishes of his parents. At the cross-road in his life, Nariman repressed his desires which stage a comeback in his dreams. Nariman's children never excused their father/ step-father for the pain that he inflicted on Yasmin through his belated chivalry in showing unbecoming consideration for Lucy to the extent of being 'the ayah's assistant.'

If poverty is one big block to the pursuit of values in their pure form at the individual level, the affluence creates impediment of another kind at the collective level for the Parsis. As mentioned earlier, the Parsi community is most concerned about its purity, a value with a lot of local import. This value has assumed importance due to the minority status of the Parsis, their number dwindling over the past few decades due mostly to the rat-race for success which marks the educated and prosperous members of the community. They feel threatened as a small island in the vast oceanic waters of a populous country. The problem is discussed by Dr. Fitter and Mr. Masalavala in a mock-serious fashion, which shows that the community does not take up the issue seriously (411-16).

The spiritual values provide sustenance to man in troubled times, but selfishness presents a stumbling block here also. This is seen in Coomy's character, who, faced with the unwelcome prospect of hosting her ailing father, invents the excuse of a leaking roof: "An act of God is no one's fault." Jal is prevailed upon to cooperate but is reportedly "uncomfortable with casting God in a supportive role in their deceitful drama" (184). In a masterstroke of poetic justice, she pays with her life for having driven "Pappa" out of her home. God does play a sporty role, however, as the 'Bombay Sporting Gods Emporium' signboard would indicate after the 'o' in 'Goods' has been blown away by storm. (370) Yezad's proposed plan is disposed of queerly by God as a real Shiv Sena man turns up in place of the fictitious one leading to the murder of an innocent Kapoor.

Yezad is flabbergasted and his guilt cries for similar reward but then it seems that God's justice is tempered with mercy; mercy because Yezad has repented. During the period of financial crunch caused by the added burden of hospital bills of his father-in-law, Yezad starts visiting the fire temple. The latter phase involving Mr. Kapoor's murder, for which he thinks himself responsible, makes this practice of visiting the *agiary* and praying there a compulsion for him. It seems to Roxana as if the entire chain of events was meant to bring Yezad to prayer (464). She feels pleased with this Yezad's new-found "faith in prayer that had descended like a blessing upon him and their house" (445). To Roxana "belief is not essential. The prayer sound itself will bring him peace and tranquillity" (445). It seems Mistry himself, much like Shakespeare in the fourth phase of his creative career, has come round to accepting the possibility of achieving divine grace through repentance and surrender. One only hopes the last creative phase of Mistry's life is long time away.

Is Yezad's surrender total? It would require deep probing, for we are entering the domain of the subconscious and the mystical. It is hardly possible for one to know one's own self fully. When it is the question of one's relationship with the Absolute, the problem becomes doubly confounded, for the Absolute hardly speaks the way He used to, in Biblical times. Even then, Job had such a difficulty resolving his doubts. It requires perhaps the sagacity of the sages of *Brihadaranyak Upanishad* to interpret the thunderous sounds. When questioned by Jehangir about the prospect of getting a new job, an unemployed Yezad's reply is, "God is great. If He wants me to, I'm sure I will" (433).

Yezad has his moments of revelation. The initial phase involving his visits to the fire temple seems to be having a salutary effect on him. The one, who hated attending to ailing Nariman for the foul smells, is now seen serving tea to him and giving him a shave. Analysing the self, he feels that the young would do well to remember death. "Carrying your death with you everyday would make it hard to waste time on unkindness and anger and bitterness, on anything petty." Also, he has the feeling that if you knew a person long enough, he could elicit every kind of emotion from you, every possible reaction, envy, admiration, pity, irritation, fury, fondness, jealousy, love, disgust. But in the end, all human beings became candidates for compassion." (358)

Yezad's metaphysical discoveries, however, come with a muddled understanding of paternal values. He hardly fits in with Jehangir's notion of a father in the family. The boy recalls the name-game that his innocent mind had invented as a child. The youngster's later point of view is authenticated through first person account in the 'Epilogue' section of the novel. Having found out the histories/meanings of the names of other members of the family, Jehangir thought that together they made a perfect family: "They were blessed, they possessed the whole world, they had their own guardian angel, and Mummy's dawn light shone upon all of them. Yet Mummy and Daddy were fighting and unhappy" (289). At that time, Yezad laughed and joked, whistled and played with the children. All that is passé. Now, "when he is home, he's either praying or reading, and says the music disturbs him" (465). Jehangir goes to the extent of observing that his real father "is gone, replaced by this non-stop-praying stranger" (500).

The fighting between Daddy and 'Pappa' (as 'Papa' is spelt throughout in this novel) is now transmuted into the one between Daddy and their elder son Murad. While Mummy "smiles contentedly" watching her husband at prayer, Murad thinks his father has "gone over the edge . . . deep into the abyss of religion" (493). Jehangir can "see and hear everything" (493); he can mark, like an insightful adult, the struggle behind the various Yashts, Gehs, Nyaishes of the prayer his father is continually muttering. Even though he has not been able to act according to the moral virtue of truth, he would very much like his sons to tread the righteous path. For this, he invokes the help of God: "O Dada Ormuzd, bless my sons, keep them healthy and honest, look after all our family according to Your will, help me do what is Your will." (437). But his younger child Jehangir is a typical new generation brat who cannot accept things as they come to him. The child's internal conflict is manifest in his longing, which seems to be the writer's as well, "If only Dada Ormuzd could help me understand! Why must prayer and religion lead to so many fights between father and son? Is that His will?" (466). Which, in effect, means our inability to translate religion beyond rituals in our life.

Looked at from another angle, Yezad's new *avtaar* as the God-fearing, constantly praying devout Parsi reminds one of Nariman's father. Is he the same Yezad who, watching the *dustoorji* in the fire-temple covering his nose and mouth was reminded of the joke about masked priests and bandits? (342). The hot blood in the veins of young Yezad has cooled down with the buffets of worldly experience. Will this history repeat itself in the case of Murad also? Yezad is sure about it because what appears fanatical to Murad is spiritual evolution to Yezad:

> "You're becoming more and more fanatical," says Murad. "I don't understand what's changing you, Daddy."
>
> "You will, as you get older. It's a spiritual evolution. You will reach a stage in your life when you too thirst for spirituality." (486)

History does repeat itself; the nuances change though. Yezad also follows the traditional path; only this conservatism seems more pronounced. This is in keeping with the mood of the times that have seen the gradual accentuation of the lines of communal division, courtesy politicians. The pictures of different apostles and prophets—Sai Baba, Virgin Mary, Christ on cross, Haji Malang, Buddha et al belonging to different faiths as also several Zarathustras used to adorn the walls of the flat in Chateau Felicity. We are told that most Parsis would love to keep these tokens of different religions in their homes. After Coomy's death, when Jal presents these to Yezad, he discusses with his orthodox friends what must be done to "non-Zarathusti images." It is decided to give them over "to the sea, to Avan Yazat, for safekeeping"—a euphemism for doing away with something that used to "interfere with the vibrations of Avesta prayers" (491).

The theme of the novel *Family Matters* reminds one of Eliot's play *The Family Reunion*. Both have some similarity as far as the title and the theme go. Harry, the central character in Eliot's play is haunted by his guilty conscience (which even takes the shape of the classical Eumanides) for his desire to kill his wife, who falls overboard a ship and gets drowned in sea waters. He ends up atoning not for his sin but for that of his father who had likewise desired to kill Harry's mother as he was infatuated by Amy's sister Agatha who restrained him in the name of the then-unborn child, viz., Harry. The *Family Matters* does not share Eliot's approach in looking at the events *a la* original sin committed by Adam for which posterity was held accountable. However, the culpability here appears more concrete even when the essential concern remains the same, i.e., the equalization of desire and deed at the site of sin.

Jehangir's is a choric comment on the futility of factitious and facile faith. He yearns for a genuinely humane order that touches the innermost depths of the self and is not confined to spaces marked by his father in the drawing room. Towards the end of the novel, he is told that post-death, all the requirements of food and clothing etc. of his grandfather would be met by Dada Ormuzd. As the first person account of Jehangir shows, he is immensely amused at the idea of this "clothing and catering service run by God." Nor does he understand the rationale of constant muttering the name of God while at the same time disregarding His creations; not attending to the cries of Nariman is a case in point. Having seen it happen before his eyes, Jehangir takes Daisy aunty's promise to perform 'a farewell concert for Nariman, made when they shifted to Chateau Felicity' (455), seriously and all alone goes out to get her from Max Mueller Bhawan when Nariman's end is suspected to be near by the doctor (469-73). This single event points to great future possibilities.

Even though ostensibly simple, the novel does deal with the complexities of life—with the vertical dimension rather than the horizontal one as in *A Fine Balance*. From the patch-quilt with a vacant corner, Mistry's leitmotif has shifted to the jigsaw puzzle that is life. In depicting life as a whole, Mistry has to take in the specifics as also the life in general, for life is an amalgam of all this and much more.

Conclusion
Reconstructing Parsi Identity

"When a culture vanishes, humanity is the loser," comments Inspector Masalawala in Rohinton Mistry's novel *Family Matters*. This concern about a progressive community with a glorious past and a dismal future underlines the writer's overzealous attempt at detailing the lifestyle and culture of the Parsis wherever he finds the opportunity in his fiction. Mistry's characters, quite commonly, represent the Parsi community, whose identity has been historically problematized. It all started with their exodus following Muslim invasion of ancient Persia which led to their settlement in the hospitable environs of Gujarat, though on condition of off-loading marginally their cultural baggage. During the British rule, they hobnobbed with the master race and got alienated from the native people. At this point, the Western lifestyle and mores permeated the Eastern inheritance of the Parsis. Post-independence, they had to adjust with the same people whom a few generations of Parsis had once learnt to deride and despise.

In recent past, another dimension has been added. A large number of young Parsis have chosen to and still continue to migrate to the West, Mistry himself being one of them, hoping to recover a life of comfort and pride. But their Western experience has reminded some of Matthew Arnold's famous lines: "Standing between two worlds, one dead/ The other powerless to be born." Rohinton Mistry's three novels, viz., *Such a Long Journey, A Fine Balance* and *Family Matters* and a collection of stories *Tales from Firozsha Baag* deal with this mixed bag of experiences, in an idiom that has ensured classic status for his works. In the case of the Indian Parsis, this identity is essentially constituted by their religious and cultural positions and practices. It also depends upon their equation with other categories of people in the society.

Since the question of cultural identity is rooted in history, the historical trajectory needs to be explored in detail here. The Parsis have had a glorious past. Theirs is one of the oldest civilizations on this earth. During those times, the force that bound the people together was located in the faith that they practised. The people of ancient Iran belonged to the Indo-European branch of the Aryans and their history goes as far back as 2000 B.C., when Zarathustra, the Prophet of ancient Iran is believed to have been born. Some of the great figures of the past whose names are etched in the minds of the Parsis are Cyrus the Great and Khushrau I also called Nowshirwan-i-Adil, i.e., Nowshirwan the Just.

In 614 A.D., Khushrau II attacked Jerusalem and captured it, killing 50000 Christians. This resulted in counter-attacks by Christian forces bringing much misery to the people. After the death of Prophet Mohammad, the Arabs started a series of invasions on Iran and were successful in. 641 A.D in capturing it. Their avowed intent was to spread their faith through force. The last king of the Persian empire Yazdegard went into hiding but after ten years he was captured and assassinated by the Muslims. The followers of Zarathustra had to flee, get converted or lie low. How the Parsis take pride in recalling their glorious past is very well shown by the words spoken on the Parsi wedding, in which the day and year is calculated from "Emperor Yazdegard of the Sassanian Dynasty of auspicious Iran . . . in accordance with the rites and rules of the Mazdayasnans" (Nanavutty 24).

The question does torment Mistry: Who is a true Parsi? He does throw up ideal characters. They have Parsi names, they pray and observe rituals the way Parsis are expected to do. Also they eat and dress in a particular way. Not all of them are ideal though. In the *Tales from Firozsha Baag*, we do meet a number of characters who need not be remembered—like Rustomji or Khorshedbai. But there is this lad Percy who grows into a thinking individual and the one who has the courage and vision to put his ideas into action and lead an authentic life. In *Such a Long Journey*, we come across Gustad Noble, who, true to his name, transcends the self and remains unshaken in his essential goodness in the face of countless vicissitudes of life—a son turning hostile, an ailing daughter, the pin-pricks of the neighbours and the unsavoury and overmuch risky adventure foisted upon him by his one-time friend Major Bilimoria. If he is shown praying in the opening scene of the novel, he is no less religious even at the end of the novel. If anything, this religiosity has taken a new meaning, for he prays "as much for Tehmul as for Jimmy. And for Dinshawji, for Pappa and Mamma, for Grandpa and Grandma, all who had had to wait for so long" (*SALJ* 337) In the end he is shown tearing the black paper off the windowpanes in a symbolic move to let into his home the light from 'outside.' There is no need for fear thereafter! That is his net gain even though poetic justice has resolved all his problems. He has realized himself and attained a kind of salvation through identifying the self with the society.

Dina Dalal in *A Fine Balance* presents the picture of a fighting female who has been wronged by destiny in the form of premature death of her loving husband. But beyond that her own brother is bent upon killing her through kindness. Dina struggles to stand on her own feet but cannot and has to come back to the condescending fold of her big brother whose wife, more than her brother Nusswan, sees to it that her position is no better than that of a domestic help. She is not the god-fearing type like Gustad but she is, nevertheless, a true Parsi who with the passing of time, transcends the worldly barriers of race, caste and creed and feels one with the tailor-turned-beggar duo Ishvar and Omprakash.

Yezad, in *Family Matters*, is not such a one who could take his place with the sublime figures talked about in the preceding paragraphs. He has yielded to the temptation and taken the devil's path. And though he realizes his mistake after it is too late, poetic justice lands him in a limbo where even constant praying does not bring peace of mind, either to him or to his near and dear ones. Jehangir notes,

> My father has emerged from the bathroom, and is doing his kusti by the cabinet. His expression is always very intense when he prays. He finishes tying the knots and sits with his prayer book before the electric afargaan, in the wooden chair no one else is allowed to use. He sits as though he is carrying a secret burden, whose weight is crushing him. He frowns a lot, his face contorting in pain. He doesn't just close his eyes, he clenches the eyelids shut, the cheeks rising, the brows pressing downwards to squeeze out whatever it is that haunts him. His Avesta recitations—the various Yashts, Gehs, Nyaishes, depending on the hour—are like a rebuttal, a protest. He is locked in a struggle. (*FM* 465)

Prayers do not reveal to him the truth that lies beyond rituals in a changed heart that does not discriminate against his son's girlfriend on the basis of her non-Parsi identity. The reaction from his son is not totally unwarranted when he fails to find the father that Yezad used to be. Perhaps Mistry wanted the Hindu businessman Kapoor, Yezad's employer, to be the ideal character. He is truly a cosmopolitan figure and in picking him, Mistry too has transcended his restricted choice of characters, for goodness knows no such bounds.

An individual could be sincere towards himself, he could hear and be answerable to his own inner voice and that would be the true authentic identity, but in the human society in which we live, the identity is known by the markers decided upon by society, for it is a mark of social recognition and import and plays a vital role in social interaction and commerce. This identity carries the burden of history and is transmuted into categories like race, creed, colour, nationality etc. There are also the markers of age, sex, vocation that are of import in day-to-day transaction of work. But when we talk about the identity, we mean by and large, the earlier set of categories. In this, as suggested, past becomes more important than even the present.

Mistry's reference to the Parsis' past is not in jingoistic terms; it is a muted one, as in the story 'Swimming Lessons' in

Tales from Firozsha Baag, in the form of the reaction of Kersi's father to his son's stories. He recounts the great figures of ancient and modern history and wishes that his son would write "something positive about Parsis." (245) More than that, Mistry's novels as also his stories are full of references to religious aspect of the Parsi life. The opening scene in *Such a Long Journey* begins with the chief character Gustad Noble offering morning prayers to the tying and untying of *kusti.* In *Family Matters*, the procedure for normal daily fire worship in an *agiary* is mentioned in detail. Again, the celebration of the *Behram roje*, the Parsi new year is the theme of the story 'One Sunday' in *Tales from the Firozsha Baag*. While *A Fine Balance* carries brief description of Dina's wedding, the detailed narration of death rituals occurs almost in each one of these works.

During the British rule in India, the western influence cast its shadow on the Parsis, who, as businessmen, felt obliged to befriend the rulers. The proximity also spilled over to the political field. Some prominent Parsi merchants helped the British rulers but the British merely used them. Apart from the British, there were also the French and the Portuguese, ruling the coastal areas. The Parsi entrepreneurs often acted as mediators between different parties. This also helped the Parsis in securing government jobs. The Christian missionaries were greatly facilitated in their work by the ruling class at that time. With the rise of the national sentiment in India, the Hindus preferred not sending their children to educational institutions run by the Christian missionaries but the Parsis did not have any such scruples with the result that their children became more proficient in English than others. The continued proximity of the Parsis to the Englishmen also created a chasm between the Parsis and other communities in India despite significant contribution made to the freedom struggle by certain towering Parsi figures like Ferozeshah Mehta, Dadabhai Naoroji, Dinshaw Wacha, Bhikaji Cama *et al.* The Parsis still continue to contribute to the national life in an impressive manner even though they comprise only 0.016% of the total population of India. Take any area—business, politics, social service, administration, professionals, armed forces, sports, science, arts, music, literature, journalism—you surely find the Parsis there.

The westernized lifestyle of the Parsis is a fact reflected in his works by Mistry also. Whether it is the surfeit of English rhymes and song-lines in *Such a Long Journey*, the birthday celebrations in *pucca* English style in *Family Matters*; the handling of love-sick Lucy by a married Professor or the way of addressing his father-in-law as 'chief' by Yezad in *Family Matters*, English culture seems to have permeated the Parsi lifestyle to a great extent. Alcohol consumption is common not only among menfolk but also among women and young boys. Thus, on the occasion of Roshan's birthday, Dilnavaz takes a few sips from her son Darius's beer glass (*SALJ* 46). The elderly lady Tehmina is hooked on to her evening scotch and soda and the Boyce family keeps its weekly supply of beef in Najamai's refrigerator (*TFFB* 26). All this shows the Parsis living in a world that is different from the common Indian way of life. Whereas this has affected their estimation in the eyes of ordinary Indians, the politico-religious turmoil in the wake of Babri demolition episode has unnerved many Parsis also. Nilufer Bharucha aptly remarks: "In decolonized India, the exalted position enjoyed by the Parsis during the Raj has been eroded and increasing dominance by the majority Hindu community has marginalized them. Parsis today are trying to reorient themselves to this new much reduced role." (Bharucha 42) To this unenviable new role can be added some other problems impinging upon their cultural identity.

The Parsis left the shores of ancient Persia for the sake of religion and have maintained their separate identity on that basis. But the modern Parsi youth, a product of western education and upbringing, is distancing himself from religion. Perhaps for this reason, Mistry has portrayed in his novels a fallen world where prayers do not usher in an equitable and humane society. The youth is particularly disenchanted as is the case with the Parsi youth Maneck Kohlah, who, in utter desperation, calls God 'the Bloody Fool' and questions his judgement of fair and foul which, according to him, is as simple as reading a balance sheet.

Says Maneck, "He would have been sacked long ago if He were managing a corporation" (*AFB* 585). The child Jehangir asks in his innocence: "If only Dada Ormuzd could help me understand! Why must prayer and religion lead to so many fights between father and son? Is that His will?" (*FM* 466). Who would give answers to such questions? The education in the Parsi religion is not organized well. At best, they have semi-literate *dustoors* or priests. There is no facility like the Sunday church school or a visiting pastor. Religious debates are unheard of. This leaves a lot to be desired from the point of view of the young generation.

Population is an important factor in the visibility and viability of any ethnic identity. Over the years, there has been a drastic fall in the population of the Parsis. The total population of the Parsis in India stood at one lakh in 1961, 90,000 in 1971 census, 75-80,000 in 1987 census (Haldar 102) and is estimated to be around 60,000 at present. Mistry is, in fact, concerned about this alarming decline in the population and is said to have stated in an interview: "when the Parsis have disappeared from the face of the earth, his writing will 'preserve a record of how they lived'" (Bharucha 45). In *Family Matters*, Dr. Fitter and Mr. Masalawala have a lively discussion on the issue of depleting numbers with the latter holding the opinion that in fifty years, there would be no Parsis left, and the former responding with a comic flair that their remains would be christened after the dinosaurs:

> "You [Jal] will be named Jalosauras," said Dr. Fitter. "I will be Shapurjisauras. If they find my father's bones, we will have a Pestonjisauras with a pugree on his head. And our inspector here, who loves his Scotch, will be the powerful
>
> "Whiskysauras, a magnum of Blue Label tucked under his arm." (*FM* 412)

Masalawala holds the 'poison' of individualism responsible for this dismal state and offers certain mock-serious solutions that fit in well with the small talk at the liquor table whereby Mistry suggests that even those who are serious about the issue are discouraged due to the lukewarm response from others in the community. Quite a few like Jal find solace in nephews and nieces rather than sons and daughters. (*FM* 417)

In fact, in an age of cut-throat competition, economic prosperity takes precedence over family. Late marriages hamper chances of sound growth. Jal and Coomy, the siblings in *Family Matters,* have not married even though they are well past their marriageable age. In this, what comes as an eye-opener is the fact that the lack of adequate housing facility in Parsi buildings and high rentals elsewhere in Bombay has also played their part (*FM* 413). Apart from it, the persona in the story 'Swimming Lessons' refers to two major problems haunting the Parsis: "We are the chosen people where osteoporosis is concerned. And divorce. The Parsi community has the highest divorce rate in India. It also claims to be the most westernized community in India. Which is the result of the other? Confusion again of cause and effect" (*TFFB* 230). With a high proportion of ageing, ailing Parsi population, the future in terms of numbers seems bleak.

While expecting the world around to change, their own house must be set in order by the Parsis. In the situation in which the community finds itself, organizations claiming to work for the community should have discharged their duties honestly and zealously in safeguarding the cultural identity and in instilling its awareness in the Parsi youth. But clearly, Mistry is not satisfied. Therefore, in his oeuvre, the work of the Parsi Panchayats and Trusts takes a drubbing. Rustomji of 'Auspicious Occasions' (*TFFB* 5) loses his cool at the very mention of the Parsi trust because it has failed to maintain well the apartment block in which he stays with his wife. One big reason for the failure of the Parsi panchayats is reported to be their hereditary character. That is certainly an anachronism in our times. The Panchayat is doing little to come to terms with the issue of falling population of the Parsis. Besides, promotion of Parsi culture and teaching of Zoroastrianism to the new generation are tasks which have to be undertaken urgently.

While safeguarding its identity, an ethnic community has also to adjust with other communities in society. It is quite normal to see stereotypes at play in this field. While the dominant community is quoted in *Such a Long Journey* as calling Parsis 'crow eaters,' the latter retaliate by referring to their liking for asafetida. Similarly, in *Tales from Firozsha Baag*, the Parsis call the natives 'ghatis' and the maidservants 'Gangas,' the dominant community members call them 'bawaji.'

While these are normal prejudices that plague mankind everywhere, a big factor that presents a hurdle to the Parsis' assimilation in the present Indian society is the Indian brand of politics. Mistry hates the political tomfoolery aimed at grabbing power through vote bank politics, at its best and through hook or crook, at its worst. There is hardly any human consideration in it. This creates aversion and distrust in the minorities. Mistry has castigated the political leadership for the ills that befell the nation in the wake of proclamation of Emergency. How this ill-advised step of the late Prime Minister Indira Gandhi affected the man in the street, has been graphically illustrated in *A Fine Balance*. Prior to it, the Nagarwala scandal during the Bangladesh liberation war proved to be Mrs. Gandhi's Achilles' heel. The plot of *Such a Long Journey* rested on it. In *Family Matters*, Mistry based the central action on the situation arising out of Shiv Sena agitation for the so-called 'sons of the soil' in Bombay. This type of political bungling presents a stumbling block in the way of the Parsis' healthy adjustment in Indian society at a time when other options like migrating to developed countries are available to them.

In these changed times, the youth—Parsis or others—particularly aspire to be world citizens, thanks to their education, skills and expanding world markets. Due to the competition from other communities in India, the Parsis have migrated in large numbers to other countries like Canada, New Zealand, Australia etc. Those who cannot make it to the promised land—Canada, in the case of Yezad in *Family Matters*—retain a life-long scar on their psyche.

Mistry has very vividly captured the mood of the Gen-next in the character of Jamshed in his story 'Lend Me Your Light'

(*TFFB*). He just cannot put up with things in Bombay and would be happy to catch the next flight back to New York. It is not necessary that the westward immigration would be successful. Even if we leave out Sarosh's 'eastern bowels, western seat' problem with its fantastic medical solutions on account of high imagination, we cannot dismiss his observation couched in oracular language that could be true of many exiles: "When you shall these unlucky deeds relate, speak of me as I am; nothing extenuate, nor set down aught in malice: tell them that in Toronto once there lived a Parsi boy as best as he could. Set you down this; and say, besides, that for some it was good and for some it was bad, but for me life in the land of milk and honey was just a pain in the posterior." (*TFFB* 168)

The issue of identity confusion is all the more severe in the case of a person living the life of an exile, for it is the case of what Derrida would call 'double displacement.' According to Derrida, "the nation is rooted first of all in the memory or anxiety of a displaced—or displaceable—population. It is not only time that is out of joint, but space, space in time, spacing." (Bharucha 55). The exile is haunted by the nostalgia of his homeland while he is hardly at home in his adopted country.

The other character in the story 'Lend Me Your Light,' Kersi is almost forced to go abroad by popular sentiment of the Parsi community including his parents. His reflection is self-reveling: "I, Tiresias, blind and throbbing between two lives, the one in Bombay and the one to come in Toronto" (*TFFB* 180). Mistry has been careful enough to juxtapose him with his brother Percy who is an idealist and risks his life to work in the rural areas of India. There are others like Kersi, who aspire but fail to make the sacrifices needed to have his elder brother's passion. He merely prays, "Lend me your light," but the likes of Percy have shunned the ambivalence and acquired an identity, not necessarily a Parsi one but surely an authentic human identity.

Bibliography

Primary Sources

Mistry, Rohinton. *Tales from Firozsha Baag*. London: Faber and Faber, 1987.

_____. *Such a Long Journey*. London: Faber and Faber, 1991

_____. *A Fine Balance*. New York: Vintage Books, 1997

_____. *Family Matters*. London: Faber and Faber, 2002

Secondary Sources

Baral, Kailash C. & Prafulla C. Kar, ed. *Identities: Local and Global*. Delhi: Pencraft International, 2003.

Bhabha, Homi K., *The Location of Culture*, London: Routledge, 1994.

_____, *Nation and Narration*, London: Routledge, 1990.

Bharucha, Nilufer, *Rohinton Mistry: Ethnic Enclosures and Transcultural Spaces*. New Delhi: Rawat Publications, 2003.

Bierstedt, Robert. *The Social Order*. New Delhi: Tata McGraw Hill, 1970.

Boyce, Mary, *Zoroastrians: The Religious Beliefs and Practices*. London: Routledge & Kegan Paul, 1979.

Bruner, Jerome, *Acts of Meaning*. Cambridge: Harvard University Press, 1990.

Chandavarkar, G.A., *Hindu Ethics*. Delhi: Chaukhamba Sanskrit Pratishthan, 2005

Chakravorty, Joya, *Indian Writing in English: Perspectives*. New Delhi: Atlantic, 2003

Chaubey, Akhilanand, *Political Consciousness and Literature*. New Delhi: Classical, 1983.

Cuddon, J.A., *A Dictionary of Literary Terms and Literary Theory*. Delhi: Maya Blackwell Doaba House, 1998.

Dahiya, Bhim Singh, *A New History of English Literature*. Delhi: Doaba, 2006.

Dadabhoy, Bakhtiar K., *Sugar in Milk: Lives of Eminent Parsis*. Delhi: Rupa.

Dallmyr, Fred, 'Social Identity and Creative Praxis,' *Identities: Local and Global*, ed. Kailash C Baral & Prafulla C. Kar. New Delhi: Pencraft International, 2003, pp. 13-30

Dass, Veena Noble & R.K. Dhawan, *Fiction of the Nineties*. Delhi: Prestige, 1994.

Dhawan, R.K., Novy Kapadia, et al, ed., *Parsi Fiction*. 2 vols. Delhi: Prestige, 2001.

Dodiya, Jaydipsinh, *The Fiction of Rohinton Mistry*. New Delhi: Prestige, 1998.

Gandhi, Leela, *Post Colonial Theory: A Critical Introduction*. Delhi: Oxford University Press, 1999.

Ginsberg, Morris. *Sociology*. Delhi: Surjeet, 1979.

Goodman, W.R., *Contemporary Literary Theory*. Delhi: Doaba, 2004.

Gupta, N.L., *A Search for Human Values*. New Delhi: Arya Book Depot, 1992.

Haldar, Santwana, ed., *Rohinton Mistry's "Such a Long Journey": A Critical Study*. New Delhi: Asia Book Club, 2006.

Haralambos, Michael. *Sociology: Themes and Perspectives*. Delhi: Oxford University Press, 1980.

Hutcheon, Linda, *A Poetics of Postmodernism: History, Theory, Fiction*. London: Routledge, 1995.

Iyenger, K.R. Srinivasa, *Indian Writing in English*. Bombay: Asia, 1962.

Kapadia, Novy, ed., *Tales from Firozsha Baag, Parsi Fiction*. Delhi: Prestige, 2001.

King, David C. & Koller, Marvin R. *Foundations of Sociology*. San Francisco: Rinehart Press, 1957.

Kulke, E, *History of the Parsis: The Minority as Agent of Social Change*. Delhi: Vikas, 1978.

Kumar, V.L.V.N. Narendra, *Parsee Novel*. Delhi: Prestige, 2002.

Kuppuswamy B., *Social Change in India*. Delhi: Konark, 1993.

Luhrmann, Tanya, *The Good Parsi: The Fate of a Colonial Elite in a Postcolonial Society*. Delhi: Oxford University Press, 1996.

Mair, Lucy, *An Introduction to Social Anthropology*. Delhi: Oxford University Press, 1997.

Madan, G.R., *Indian Social Problems*. New Delhi: Allied, 1997.

Morey, Peter, *Rohinton Mistry*. London: Manchester University Press, 2004.

Nanavutty, Piloo. 1980. *The Parsis*. New Delhi: National Book Trust.

Nayar, Pramod, *Literary Theory Today*. New Delhi: Asia Book Club, 2002.

Naik, Chanchala K., 'Identity and the Social Self,' *Identities: Local and Global*, ed. Kailash C. Baral, et al. New Delhi: Pencraft International, 2003, pp. 65-77

Naik, M.K. & Shyamala A. Narayan, *Indian English Literature 1980-2000: A Critical Survey*. Delhi: Pencraft International, 2007.

Nehru, Jawaharlal, *The Discovery of India*. New Delhi: Jawaharlal Nehru Memorial Fund, Impression 2003.

Pandit, Dr. Balkrishna S., *Western Philosophy (Metaphysics)*. Delhi: SBD, 2001.

Paul, S.L., *Philosophical Background to Western Literature*. Karnal: Sidhartha, 1989.

Petrovsky A.V. & Yarosthevsky M.G., *A Concise Psychological Dictionary*. Moscow: Progress Publishers 1985.

Radhakrishnan, S., *Recovery of Faith*..Delhi: Orient Paperbacks, 1967.

Richards, I.A. 'Pseudo Statements,' *Twentieth Century Criticism: The Major Statements*. Ed. William J. Handy & Max Westbrook. New Delhi: Light & Life Publishers, 1976.

Ridley, M.R. *Othello*. London: Methuen, 1969.

Roy, Anjali Gera & Meena T. Pillai, *Rohinton Mistry: An Anthology of Recent Criticism*. Delhi: Pencraft International, 2007.

Rushdie, Salman, *Imaginary Homelands*. London: Granta Books, 1992.

Russell, Bertrand, *Human Society in Ethics and Politics*. London: George Allen & Unwin, 1954.

Rutherford, Jonathan, *Identity: Community, Culture, Difference*. London: Lawrence and Wishart, 1990.

Shaw, George Bernard. *Man and Superman*. Middlesex: Penguin, 1977, p. 251.

Sheikh, Narmeen, Interview with Rohinton Mistry, www.asiasource.com, Dec. 18, 2007.

Thornton, Fr. James. *Vilfred Pareto: A Concise Overview of His Life, Works and Philosophy*. www.google.com

Thilly, Frank. *A History of Philosophy*. New Delhi: SBW, 2005.

Trivedi, Harish, *Colonial Transactions: English Literature and India*. Calcutta: Papyrus, 1993.

Wadia, Hutoxi, *Shade of Indian Modernity in the Novels of Rohinton Mistry*. Delhi: Pencraft International, 2000.